Praise for

THE BLACK MADONNA

*"A sumptuous, multi-layered manifesto on the adoration of the Sacred Black Feminine, **Christena Cleveland's** The Black Madonna invites the reader onto a literary pilgrimage to meet Black Madonnas of the world. This book reminds those who are under-mothered that Black Madonna has always been with us, nourishing us through her sacred womb. It is a triumphant prayer pronouncing the ever-loving, ever-compassionate ability of Black Madonna to replenish, give us breath, protect, soothe pain, and ensure our freedom once we come to her. In a world that is tearing at its seams, Cleveland insists that it is the love of Black Madonna that will save us all."*

— **Natasha Gordon-Chipembere, PhD,** professor of African diasporic literature at Long Island University and author of *Finding La Negrita*

*"**Christena Cleveland** has journeyed courageously into the depths of healing and returned with a map forged from her own evolution. In* The Black Madonna, *she places powerful cartographic tools in our hands, inviting us to chart our own paths toward spiritual liberation in the company of the sacred Black feminine. Cleveland's work has always been impactful; here, it is lush, lyrical, and profoundly transformative."*

— **Dr. Chanequa Walker-Barnes,** professor of practical theology and pastoral care at Columbia Theological Seminary and author of *Too Heavy a Yoke*

*"The Black Madonna is a gift to anyone craving a divine feminine spirituality— but especially to 'under-mothered' Black women, socialized to cast our own needs aside and nurture everyone else. As Black women navigate transgenerational burdens—enslavement, white supremacy, misogynoir—we find in Black Madonna not only solace but our own holiness as well. In the tradition of bell hooks, who longed for Black liberation via the sacred Black feminine, **Christena Cleveland** calls readers to unshackle themselves from religions of domination. Whether tracing history or describing personal encounters, Cleveland's book is a revelation—one that Black people, too often denigrated and devalued, sorely need."*

— **Nadra Nittle,** author of *bell hooks' Spiritual Vision*

*"**Christena Cleveland** has written a revolutionary, indispensable, brilliant, and achingly original book. She has opened us to the love field of the Black Madonna in a way that restores us to our original inheritance and divine presence in life. Cleveland's work will permanently transform our understanding and help us birth ourselves in the middle of this global dark night into midwives of the Black Madonna's reality of justice and love."*

— **Andrew Harvey,** author of *The Magdalene Revolution*

THE
BLACK
MADONNA

ALSO BY CHRISTENA CLEVELAND, PhD

God Is a Black Woman

Disunity in Christ: Uncovering the Hidden Forces That Keep Us Apart

Please visit:

Hay House USA: www.hayhouse.com®
Hay House Australia: www.hayhouse.com.au
Hay House UK: www.hayhouse.co.uk
Hay House India: www.hayhouse.co.in

THE BLACK MADONNA

ICON OF RESISTANCE & NOURISHER OF SOULS

CHRISTENA CLEVELAND, PhD

HAY HOUSE LLC

Carlsbad, California • New York City
London • Sydney • New Delhi

Copyright © 2026 by Christena Cleveland

Published in the United States by:
Hay House LLC, www.hayhouse.com®
P.O. Box 5100, Carlsbad, CA, 92018-5100

Cover art: Laylie Frazier
Cover design: Faceout Studio, Molly von Borstel
Interior design: Karim J. Garcia

All rights reserved. No part of this book may be reproduced by any mechanical, photographic, or electronic process, or in the form of a phonographic recording; nor may it be stored in a retrieval system, transmitted, or otherwise be copied for public or private use—other than for "fair use" as brief quotations embodied in articles and reviews—without prior written permission of the publisher.

The author of this book does not dispense medical advice or prescribe the use of any technique as a form of treatment for physical, emotional, or medical problems without the advice of a physician, either directly or indirectly. The intent of the author is only to offer information of a general nature to help you in your quest for emotional, physical, and spiritual well-being. In the event you use any of the information in this book for yourself, the author and the publisher assume no responsibility for your actions.

Tradepaper ISBN: 979-8-3186-0186-6
E-book ISBN: 979-8-3186-0187-3
Audiobook ISBN: 979-8-3186-0188-0

1st Printing

Printed in the United States of America

This product uses responsibly sourced papers, including recycled materials and materials from other controlled sources.

The authorized representative in the EU for product safety and compliance is Penguin Random House Ireland, Morrison Chambers, 32 Nassau Street, Dublin D02 YH68, Ireland. https://eu-contact.penguin.ie

*For bell hooks
who urged African Americans to reclaim Black Madonna
as an icon of resistance and nourisher of souls*

CONTENTS

INVOCATION

Holy Insurrectionist, you love to stir shit up.
So when the murky dust settles,
We see that everything this colonial world
Has conditioned us to build is simply trash.

Empire Assassin, you lovingly topple our inner empires—
The internalized lies that keep us small
and tethered to the plantation economy,
Too scared to step out and into your blessed fugitivity.

Divine Ancestor, we are cut from your cloth.
Show us that we're too sacred for this
Little life of resource scarcity and self-doubt.
Override our conditioning with your regal DNA.

Icon of Resistance, your Black body is a gospel
Proclaiming that Blackness is holy and femininity is divine.
Since you cannot be shamed, tamed, or contained,
We lift our heads as we burst forth in you.

North Star, Our Lady of Liberation,
By your light we see our next bold step.
As you usher in a world of true freedom.
May we be holy and stir shit up too.

Chapter 1

SHE SPARKS OUR LIBERATION

Following Black Madonna into Deeper Freedom

As a Black American whose ancestors were enslaved, I often wonder what possessed some enslaved people to risk everything, choose freedom above all else, and revolt against an overwhelmingly powerful plantation society. I don't have access to specific historical details about my ancestors. But in my daydreams, I like to imagine my mythical ancestor awakening one seemingly ordinary day, getting dressed, anointing her radiant ebony skin with oil, and gently brushing her glorious 4c black hair. Then, while exiting her plantation cabin and surveying the glistening sun rising above the milky cotton fields, my ancestor simply shakes her head and steadfastly declares to herself, "I'm too sacred for this."

Our enslaved Black ancestors were socially and religiously programmed to remain dutifully oppressed for their entire lives. The mere physical and emotional brutality of slavery practically forced them to disconnect from their bodies, emotions, and desires, thus making it nearly impossible for them to connect with the deep, embodied wisdom that lovingly whispers, "You're too sacred for this." As somatic practitioner Kelsey Blackwell writes, "Our people . . . learned to push our anger down, to disconnect from feeling and sensation 'to get through,' to not take up too much space, to always be helping, to apologize for ourselves and our bodies."[1]

Despite all odds, a rare few of our enslaved ancestors incited rebellions. What gave them the audacity? What empowered them to believe they were worthy of freedom? In a wicked colonial society that was designed to tether and diminish them, what sparked their liberation?

As I began to study the early slave rebellions in colonial America, I discovered that perhaps the question isn't *what* sparked their liberation, but *who* sparked their liberation.

BLACK MADONNA: ICON OF RESISTANCE

Not surprisingly, they don't teach much about slave rebellions in high school history class; like many of us who want to learn Black history, I had to educate myself. And tragically, I was well into adulthood when I first learned about the Stono Rebellion of 1739, which, according to historian Henry Louis Gates Jr., was the largest slave rebellion ever staged in the 13 colonies. This epic and costly pre–Revolutionary War slave revolt was orchestrated by Kongolese Catholics who, like my mythical ancestor, believed that they were simply too sacred for slavery. But unlike my mythical ancestor, we have access to historical details that reveal that an uncommon dark-skinned version of the Virgin Mary named Black Madonna was the *who* that fueled this particularly iconic rebellion.

Like many other enslaved people, the Kongolese were subjected to religious and social programming that tried to convince them that they were unworthy of freedom. On the American plantation, enslaved Africans were systematically stripped of their ancestral languages, customs, and spiritualities and forced to assimilate to the values of the plantation—namely, the English language, absolute subservience to white masters and the norms of the plantation, and allegiance to the white jesus* of the plantation, who shared

---

*Historians agree that the historical Jesus of Nazareth was of African and Asian descent and likely resembled a modern-day Arab man. The concept of a "white Jesus" is a figment of the colonial imagination, a lie invented to uphold white supremacy. (For more, see Chapter 2 of my book *God Is a Black Woman*.) For this reason, I use lowercase letters when I refer to the white jesus of the plantation.

the same race as their captors and affirmed the enslaved people's diminished status. Yet when the Kongolese learned that the Spanish promised emancipation to any enslaved people who escaped to St. Augustine, Florida, they began planning their revolt and journey toward freedom.

On the weekend of September 8, 1739, the Kongolese strategically waited until their masters were preoccupied at church before adorning themselves in blazing white attire, then collected their sacred ancestral drums and raided a firearms store near the Stono River about 20 miles southwest of Charleston, South Carolina. Once armed, they began their valiant rebellion. "With cries of 'Liberty' and beating of drums," historian Peter H. Wood writes, "the rebels raised a standard and headed south toward Spanish St. Augustine . . . Along the road they gathered Black recruits, burned houses, and killed white opponents."[2] Over the course of several miles, the group of revolutionaries grew to almost 60 people, and over 20 white slave owners were killed, primarily by beheading.

Astoundingly, the clothing, drumming, and even the date that the revolutionaries selected for their rebellion point to Black Madonna as the source of empowerment and inspiration. According to historian Mark M. Smith, the Kongolese wore white in honor of Black Madonna, who is often associated with the color, played drums in homage to the sacred rhythms at Black Madonna's cathedral in the Kingdom of Kongo, and even carried out the attack on the annual feast day of Black Madonna.[3]

When I take a moment to immerse myself in the Kongolese freedom journey, I am astounded. Despite the forceful colonial programming, they somehow resisted; excavated their deep, embodied wisdom; faced their terror; relinquished their colonial attachments; and charted a liberation path. As they were enslaved people, life off the plantation was likely a complete mystery to them. They probably had no personal knowledge of the terrain or the environmental threats—like hostile white people, animal predators, and inhospitable fauna and flora—that could harm them. They had no idea whether their escape attempt would be successful or whether it would end in their capture and death by flogging. Even if they successfully escaped, they couldn't have known whether the skills they acquired on the plantation would transfer to the free world and secure a living for them. Even more, if they found themselves in a desperate situation, they couldn't have known whom to trust and whom to be wary of, because people of any race, even other Black folks, could be spies for plantation owners. On a relational note, they couldn't have known what would happen to the loved ones they left behind on the plantation, and perhaps they trembled at the thought. In truth, no amount of reconnaissance and careful planning could reduce the enormous risk that lay in their trek toward freedom.

In the midst of all the body-shuddering unknowns, the Kongolese took a deep breath, embraced their intrinsic sacredness, and marched off the plantation. Though the path to freedom was perilous and unpredictable, they implicitly understood that they were not alone; they were accompanied by a trustworthy and abundant protector who was deeply invested in their wellness and liberation. Despite the colonizers' ardent attempts to disempower them, the Kongolese revolutionaries were empowered by Black Madonna and knew that they were worthy of freedom. They were connected to a cosmic truth that their sacredness required their freedom, a cosmic truth that powerfully overrode the earthly realities of the plantation.

With Black Madonna guiding and reassuring them, the Kongolese revolutionaries could face anything.

ARE WE TALKING ABOUT THE SAME MARY?

Now, you might be thinking, *But wait—isn't Black Madonna (aka the Virgin Mary) a relic of Christianity? And isn't Christianity the religion of the plantation? How did the Kongolese know of Black Madonna— and more importantly, how did she liberate and empower them to resist the plantation?*

Though we often assume that Christianity was introduced to Africans *after* colonial enslavement, groundbreaking work by historians such as David Daniels unveils the truth that many African communities practiced a version of Christianity while still living on their ancestral lands.[4] Prior to the transatlantic slave trade, the Portuguese established Catholicism in the Kongo, and many Kongolese made magic by integrating the most life-giving aspects of Catholicism with their Indigenous spiritualities. Specifically, many Kongolese Catholics nurtured a deep devotion to the Virgin Mary, elevating her beyond her diminished status as an unassuming and relatively powerless "servant of God" to co-chief of Christ and a goddess in her own right. Despite the patriarchal teachings of the Catholic Church, the Kongolese drew upon an Indigenous cosmology that affirmed the divine power of women and embraced the Virgin Mary as an emboldened Christ figure who possessed all the powers and grace that Jesus and the Father possessed. They implicitly understood what Black Madonna devotee Mirabai Starr would teach over 250 years later: She is ". . . the quintessential Mother, the feminine face of the Holy One, fierce protector and gentle consoler . . . She refuses to be defined as the passive, obedient handmaid of the Father. She is the radical, powerful, engaged Mother of the World."[5]

But to the Kongolese, the Virgin Mary was so expansive and compelling that she couldn't be fully defined by or confined to Christianity; she was also venerated as a Kongolese ancestor. As Smith writes, "Beyond the Kongolese commitment to Catholicism generally, evidence suggests that the Virgin Mary occupied an important place in their cosmology."[6] As both a Christ figure *and* an ancestor, the Virgin Mary of the Kongolese was explicitly African. For example, in 1704 back in the Kongo, Dona Beatriz Cimpa Vita, a young Kongolese anti-colonial revolutionary, decried the racism of the Catholic Church and audaciously took it upon herself to revise the official church prayers to affirm that "Jesus and Mary were actually Kongolese" and that Mary could be reliably called upon when Kongolese people experienced colonial violence.[7] Unlike the distant, porcelain white Mary of European Christianity, the Kongolese Virgin Mary was Black Madonna—a Black version of the Virgin Mary who relates to the unique experiences of Black people and reliably stands with us as a powerful advocate against racial oppression and the other colonial powers. Since Black Madonna was both their holy queen and their ancestor, her very existence affirmed the Kongolese's divine birthright as cherished and sacred human beings. As members of her lineage, the Kongolese knew they were divine too, and far too worthy for life on the plantation. No amount of colonial programming could dissuade them from the liberating truth they encountered in Black Madonna.

Though the Stono Rebellion was the largest slave rebellion in early colonial America, it was unsuccessful in a purely physical sense. Once the local militia was alerted, it quickly mobilized and engaged the revolutionaries in a field near the Jacksonborough ferry. Though the revolutionaries fought valiantly, more than half of them were killed before they could escape, and most of the ones who escaped were hunted down and beheaded. Nevertheless, the Stono Rebellion sparked a series of slave revolts around colonial America. As news of the Stono Rebellion spread, many other enslaved people began to embody their sacredness in a new way and seek freedom for themselves. In a cosmic sense, the Stono revolutionaries—with their unforgettable white attire, sacred drumming, and fearless beheadings—liberated the imaginations of countless enslaved people who could now echo their cry for liberty.

I am astonished that in a colonial world ruled by white supremacy and its patron saint, white jesus, the Kongolese devotion to Black Madonna clothed them in sacredness, inoculated them from the forceful colonial conditioning that claimed they were worthy only of enslavement, and fortified their efforts for liberty. Despite the towering uncertainty that surrounded them, the Kongolese embraced the cosmic truth that Black Madonna teacher Clarissa Pinkola Estés would affirm centuries later, about "how deeply incubated we are in the Holy Mother, we, the children of the dark-skinned holy woman who is never afraid of the dark."[8] Black Madonna was their North Star, and with Black Madonna guiding them, they could face anything. Through the Stono Rebellion, Black Madonna nourished generations of enslaved Black people to embody their sacredness, find their North Star, and get free. Even more, I was astounded when I learned that right around the time of the Stono Rebellion, Black Madonna was also inspiring revolution among enslaved Africans in Haiti. In this book, as we explore resistance efforts throughout the African diaspora, we'll come to see that Black Madonna is a holy insurrectionist who is known for empowering radical freedom. We'll come to see that Black Madonna is often the *who* that sparks liberation.

RECLAIMING BLACK MADONNA

As the heroic story of the Kongolese revolutionaries reveals, Black Madonna is an irreplaceable icon of resistance for Black people, one that can withstand and transform even the most vile colonial environments. Yet tragically, most Black people have never heard of her, much less been emancipated by her. For example, though I was deeply engaged in both Christian and racial justice communities throughout my young adult life, I didn't learn of Black Madonna until I was in my mid-30s. In all honesty, if I hadn't intentionally gone looking for her, I doubt I would have found her. Amid the awakenings of the #BlackLivesMatter and #MeToo movements and the sickening backwash of Trump's 2016 election, I began desperately seeking a divine being who could relate to my experiences as a Black person and as a woman. It only took one quick Google search for me to discover Black Madonna—a sacred Black feminine being who has existed for millennia yet often remains hidden in plain sight. As we'll come to uncover in this book, though Black Madonna is often associated with the Catholic Church, her roots are much deeper than Catholicism and go back to ancient Black goddesses like Isis of Egypt, Black Artemis of ancient Ephesus (Turkey), and Cybele of ancient Phrygia (Turkey). Neither tamed nor contained by Catholicism, the wild, loving, and fierce Black Madonna draws seekers from all religious and spiritual paths, including African American Hoodoo, Afro-Brazilian Candomblé, and Afro-Cuban Santería. Further, much like the Kongolese, Black and brown people around the globe and across the centuries have found refuge, hope, healing, and liberation among the more than 450 Black Madonnas that currently exist in Africa, North America, South America, Asia, and Europe. Though the different Black Madonnas around the world have unique names and culturally rooted stories, they collectively represent one unitary and powerful being. But this vast interspiritual and diasporic history was unknown to me as an African American with deep roots in the Protestant church.

Even after I encountered Black Madonna, I felt almost entirely alone as a Black devotee. Almost all the research and teachings on Black Madonna that I found were written by white people who essentially ignored her Black racial identity. To them, Black Madonna's Blackness has to do with her ethereal nature, her connection to the earth, and her connection to the underworld. In other words, Black Madonna's Blackness has nothing to do with her Black body and her identification with Black people. White scholars have even gone so far as to actively deny her Black racial identity, claiming that Black Madonnas are really just white Madonnas that have been darkened over the years by candle soot. As it has so many other things, whiteness has colonized Black Madonna.

It wasn't until years into my journey toward Black Madonna that I learned that iconic Black feminist bell hooks was also a devotee of Black Madonna and was deeply sustained by her. In her book *Homegrown*, hooks details her first encounter with Black Madonna while in college. She writes, "In my life, I've traveled all over the world to see beautiful art. But my pilgrimage to the Shrine of the Black Madonna in Montserrat [Spain] nourished my soul. This image of a beautiful, dark Madonna, blessing and healing the world is counterhegemonic: it challenges the equation of Blackness with ugliness." Later hooks lamented the fact that most Black Americans remain unaware of and are even resistant to Black Madonna, saying, "Unfortunately, African Americans have not been interested in reclaiming representations of [B]lack Madonnas. . . . And this is a sensitive point because most constructions of Black[ness] are tied to representations that are hateful and ugly, so that the idea of an icon that can stand in resistance becomes further and further away."[9] To hooks, Black Madonna uniquely nourishes Black souls, invites Black people to embody our sacredness, and offers herself as an icon of resistance to all the ways that our modern-day plantation society tries to make us feel like we are unworthy and powerless. In fact, hooks biographer Nadra Nittle affirms, "hooks posited that images of the Dark Virgin could inspire Black Americans just as they have for other groups such as Indigenous Mexicans and Afro-descendants throughout the Americas . . . as bearer[s] of the sacred, the healing, the inspiring."[10]

When I learned that our ancestor bell hooks wants us to reclaim and embrace Black Madonna as an icon of resistance for Black people, I began to scour the global and historical world for stories that, told through a Black lens, affirm and empower Black people. I didn't have to look far. As I dug beneath the surface of the official church and historical records and talked to regular people who are devoted to Black Madonna, I uncovered countless rarely publicized, heartwarming, empowering, and often hilarious stories about her that show us who she truly is. As we'll see throughout this book, despite what the white scholars say, Black Madonna is undeniably Black and consistently sides with and emancipates the oppressed, the silenced, the enslaved, the cast out, and the disempowered. Visual artist and Black Madonna scholar Justin Randolph Thompson agrees, asserting that the vast majority of Black Madonnas are, "despite policing and negation, unapologetically and distinctly Black beyond speculation."[11]

Before we begin our illuminating exploration of Black Madonna, I want to point out that this book differs from most books on Black Madonna in three crucial ways:

First, I have intentionally centered the Black experience and focused on how Black Madonna empowers and liberates Black people across the diaspora. Though all people of all races are truly welcome as Black Madonna kin, throughout the book I've sought out and prioritized the voices and perspectives of Black artists, scholars, teachers, and devotees. I did this to honor hooks's ancestral call for Black people to reclaim Black Madonna, as well as to honor Black Madonna's Black body and disrupt the white supremacist norms that rule many spiritual spaces.

Second, in order to help us not just *know* things about Black Madonna but also *experience* her, I've included invocations to begin each chapter and embodied practices that end each chapter. These are designed to nurture an authentic connection with Black Madonna, who longs to commune with us.

Third, in order to honor Black Madonna's deeply relational and imminent nature, I have chosen not to refer to her as "the Black Madonna," which feels like a distant title to me. Instead, I have omitted "the" and simply call her "Black Madonna," which, from my perspective, fosters intimacy. The exception is when I refer to a specific Black Madonna by her official title (e.g., the Black Madonna of Paris), as we'll see in the unforgettable story that follows.

OUR LADY OF FUCK AROUND AND FIND OUT

The Black Madonna of Paris, who is also called Our Lady of Good Deliverance, is a superstar Black Madonna. Since she burst onto the scene in the 11th century, her extra-dark-chocolate skin; bright red lips; elegant, voluminous red-white-and-blue robe; and fleur-de-lis scepter, which connotes her status as royalty, have drawn millions of devotees. With her afro-puffed child resting on her left hip, Our Lady of Good Deliverance stands tall and firmly rooted at the center altar of the convent chapel of the Congregation of the Sisters of St. Thomas of Villeneuve just outside Paris. On my first visit to her, I entered the small and unassuming chapel and was both enticed and comforted by Black Madonna's intensely serene gaze that appears to look directly at the realities of the world and yet remains unfazed. It's no wonder that she is called Our Lady of Good Deliverance; her entire vibe is so grounded and stable that it seems that literally nothing in the world can steal her peace or the peace that she offers to those who seek it. Who better to approach when one is in desperate need of a good deliverance?

Given her status as the oldest existing Black Madonna in Paris, it's not surprising that many famous luminaries have been drawn to her. Countless French kings and queens, as well as important Parisian saints such as Vincent de Paul and Francis de Sales, are among her celebrity devotees. According to the official church records, she is called Our Lady of Good Deliverance because across the medieval and Renaissance periods, she was especially known for miraculously helping women safely deliver their babies in an era when childbirth was especially dangerous. And yet, if you talk to Black Madonna lovers across France, you'll hear an entirely different story about why she is called Our Lady of Good Deliverance.

According to the unofficial oral tradition, the Black Madonna of Paris has been known for helping women in abusive marriages get free. For centuries women in France were so disempowered that they were unable to divorce their husbands, even if their husbands were abusing them. With the law and Church doctrine against them, they literally had nowhere to turn when they feared for their lives and the lives of their children.

So they sought help from Our Lady of Good Deliverance.

For hundreds of years, abused women all over the countryside would set out on foot toward Paris—braving the elements, crossing snowcapped mountain ranges, and evading bandits in order to pray at the altar of the Black Madonna of Paris. According to the stories that I've heard dozens of times from dozens of people in dozens of different French villages, whenever a woman asked Our Lady of Good Deliverance to free her from her abusive husband, he would magically disappear. In other words, he was never seen or heard from again. No body, no crime scene, no nothing. Just gone.

I'm not saying she killed him but . . .

Clearly, Our Lady of Good Deliverance knows how to handle her business.

Like countless Black women I know and love, when Black Madonna is given a task, you can consider it handled. She is the cosmic embodiment of the "trust Black women" mantra that is commonly shared on social media. Beyond her divine trustworthiness lies an unbothered steadfastness that is not subject to the systems of this world. Like most Black women, she knows how to "make a way out of no way." And if oppressors fuck with Our Lady of Good Deliverance or the marginalized folks she loves, they will swiftly find out exactly how good she is at making a way out of no way. That's why I've nicknamed her Our Lady of Fuck Around and Find Out. Behind her intense and serene Black feminine gaze lies a strategic knowledge of how to work around the systems of oppression so that all who should be free can, in fact, be free. When the law of the land and the moral authority stand against liberation, she invites the most disempowered to her altar to tell their stories and receive her unflappable peace. We can trust that Our Lady of Fuck Around and Find Out is going to handle it.

More than anything, the stories about Our Lady of Good Deliverance illuminate who she is and what she means to the most marginalized people. In a society in which abusers are protected rather than held accountable, in which victims are terrorized and silenced, in which even the police and church are agents of oppression, the people know without a shadow of a doubt that Our Lady of Fuck Around and Find Out will hear them and trust their eyewitness accounts. Many divine icons, such as white jesus, have been stripped of their liberatory powers, removed from their historical allegiance with the oppressed, co-opted by colonialism, and transformed into agents of oppression. Yet Our Lady of Good Deliverance remains united in solidarity with the oppressed. She stands defiantly and serenely in her chapel in Paris, helping people who haven't held the mic in years find their voice and boldly tell their story, and actively intervening in support of their liberation. And to the abusers who are accustomed to avoiding accountability, Our Lady of Fuck Around and Find Out embodies the divine being that the historical Mary, the mother of Jesus, described in the Gospel of Luke: "You have scattered the proud in their conceit; you have deposed the mighty from their thrones and raised the lowly to high places." Or, as Black women say to abusers, "Fuck around and find out."

SHE CHANGES *EVERYTHING*

As someone who has been a Black Madonna devotee and student for years, I'm not surprised that the most disempowered women turned to the Black Madonna of Paris to help them reclaim their worth and voice in a society that hammered them with unworthiness and silencing. I'm also not surprised that the Kongolese who orchestrated the iconic Stono Rebellion that inspired generations of enslaved people were inspired by Black Madonna. And again, it's no surprise that bell hooks's iconic Black feminist leadership, which has awakened countless Black people to the ways in which we can be more free, was inspired by her early, powerful, face-to-face encounter with Black Madonna. My first encounter with Black Madonna in 2016 instantly empowered me to become aware of the ways in which my Black, embodied soul remained shackled to modern-day plantations and longed to be free.

In the span of one tempestuous January afternoon, I was transfigured. In order to retrieve a delivery of books on Black Madonna, I had just braved the windy and rainy inferno that lay between my porch and the cavernous mailbox at the end of my long gravel driveway. After I dried off, I made a cup of cinnamon cardamom tea and settled into the nest of blankets on my kitchen couch. Before studying the text, I decided to casually flip through the books and peruse the illustrations of the Great Black Mother within. And that's when the shift began. Before I even read anything, my soul immediately recognized that the photos and drawings of ancient Black Madonnas affirmed my questions about my own sacredness as a Black person.

Growing up as a Black evangelical Christian, I was often taught that "I was fearfully and wonderfully made" (Psalm 139:14) and deeply loved by God. Yet due to the overwhelming number of white jesus images that litter the modern-day plantation that we call America, as well as the overwhelmingly denigrating ways our society *treats* Black people, I struggled to claim and embody my Black sacredness. Throughout my young adulthood, I would often ask myself:

If I truly am sacred, then why don't I listen to, much less trust, my inner knowing? Why do I always need to look outside myself for wisdom and guidance?

If I truly am sacred, then why do I still question my intrinsic beauty?

If I truly am sacred, then why do I still seek to control myself and others? Why can't I trust my body's wisdom and affirm other people's body wisdom?

If I truly am sacred, then why are so many of my relationships transactional, rife with jealousy, and governed by our competitive, capitalist system?

If I truly am sacred, then why do I still hold myself to an impossible standard of perfection?

If I truly am sacred, then why do I still carry so much fear about what will happen to me if I reject what society has taught me about who I should be and what I need to do in order to stay alive?

If I truly am sacred, then why do I stay in toxic relationships and professional communities that cannot hold me with care?

But the thousand-year-old Black Madonnas depicted in the books in front of me liberated my questions with the force of a cork popping off a bottle of champagne. No longer buried, they burst forth so forcefully, so viscerally, so permanently that I would have been frightened had I not been unexpectedly certain that these questions would not stimulate destabilizing ambiguity. I knew they would stimulate empowering freedom. Like my mythical ancestor, I was awakening to the truth that *I am simply too sacred for this.*

The fiercely kind images of Black Madonna showed me that my questions are not only valid but are harmonious echoes of questions heard around the globe and across time. Within a matter of minutes, I went from being a Black woman woefully disconnected from her sacredness to one who was eager to seek wholeness and freedom at all costs. Like the Kongolese revolutionaries, I had found the *who* that sparked my liberation.

There was just one enormous problem: I had been so deeply programmed by our modern-day plantation society that I didn't quite know how to be free. My identity, source of power, and sense of stability all lay within the plantation system. The plantation was all I knew; I had no idea how to navigate my way off the plantation. At the time of my awakening to Black Madonna, I was a professor at Duke Divinity School and the first Black American and first female director of the Duke Center for Reconciliation. I had essentially been hired to make Duke, an institution that was funded by money made from slave labor, seem less racist than it actually is. As such, I spent a good chunk of my day cleaning up white people's messes. When the racism of Duke and its institutional partners was exposed, I was called in to make a very public but very toothless speech about "love" and the "beloved community" in an effort to improve their image. Bearing the hulking, thorny crown of the "reconciler," I went from conference stage to conference stage, institution to institution, and pulpit to pulpit—dutifully sanitizing the facade of racist white organizations that had zero intention of changing and treated me like the house nigger they perceived me to be. Though my work as a "reconciler" traumatized me—ultimately, leading my digestive system to completely shut down—I genuinely felt that it was my duty to "be the bridge," to sacrifice my own well-being for others . . . because isn't that what Jesus did on the cross?

Whenever I questioned my work on the reconciliation plantation, I was immediately pointed back to conservative Christian theology, in which self-sacrifice is the hallmark of love and holiness. As theologian and psychologist Chanequa Walker-Barnes explains, "The Christian understanding of love as self-sacrifice and self-denial trains women for a form of 'theological masochism,' in which women learn to accept, submit to, and sometimes even welcome unjust suffering because such suffering is thought to be their divinely ordained role."[12] In the Christian communities of my roots, I was taught that being useful to others, even at one's own expense, is the pathway to true significance.

Regrettably, I internalized this teaching and even fortified it in the course of my academic work. In a term paper for a doctoral philosophy class on the self, I argued that according to the teachings of Jesus, the most noble self is actually the absence of self. I believed that to be a faithful follower of Christ meant to have no needs, no voice, no perspective, and no identity of my own. Though I initially received this message during childhood, I also received it as an adult. Throughout my public-facing career, I was repeatedly told that I was a modern-day Queen Esther, a reference to the Old Testament woman who was kidnapped, imprisoned, sex-trafficked, and repeatedly raped by a maniacal emperor in order for her people to be set free. In this horrific story, which is often glorified in the conservative Christian world, Esther's self-sacrificial suffering was the key to her people's liberation. Between the images of the Suffering Christ on the cross and of Queen Esther, it's no wonder my body eventually quit on me. My spirituality was literally the opposite of that of the Kongolese, who unabashedly believed that their sacredness *required* their freedom. Their spirituality affirmed that they were simply too sacred for plantation life, and it empowered them to seek liberation—no matter the cost.

YOU'RE WITH ME NOW—AND I'M HANDLING IT

I desperately longed to internalize my sacred Blackness as the Kongolese had, so not long after I awakened to Black Madonna I spent seven days on a walking pilgrimage in the woods of the historic Stagville Plantation just north of Durham, North Carolina. Based on my research, I knew Black Madonna cared deeply about my liberation as a Black person, and I wanted to create space for her to mystically speak to me as she had to the Kongolese. Like them, I wanted her to inspire me to audaciously revise the "official" Christian texts so that they affirmed my Black sacredness. Like the Kongolese, I wanted to experience her as a divine liberator and an ancestor, and I wanted her to speak to me as I walked miles and miles and miles on the land that held the blood, sweat, and tears of my ancestors.

While driving to Stagville Plantation for the first day of my walking pilgrimage, I took a wrong turn. I almost never drove north of Durham because I don't love Confederate flags, and they seemed to abound up there among the wooded Carolina homesteads that lie between Durham and the Virginia state line. Prior to my walking pilgrimage, I only ventured north of Durham in order to teach my weekly class on justice and leadership at Butner Federal Prison. Having made the drive to Butner numerous times, I absentmindedly turned right toward the prison instead of left toward the historic plantation. It was a reasonable mistake; the two vast properties are just a short walk from each other. Their proximity taunted me, painfully illuminating the lineage between plantations and prisons.

It had recently rained, and as I walked Stagville's flooded, muddy fields, I thought about my incarcerated students at Butner. Their earnestness. Their beautiful Black and brown faces. And their shame. I remembered how, during our first discussion of the racist reality of mass incarceration, these men desperately pushed back, insisting that their imprisonment was solely due to their vile natures. Unacquainted with their sacred Blackness, they gravely assured me that they deserve to be "criminals" and that their sentencing at Butner had nothing to do with race. Later in the semester, we talked about internalized oppression and internal light bulbs illuminated as they learned that humans can begin to believe the lies that an unjust society tells them about their intrinsic goodness, worth, and rights. But at first, they were completely unaware that they had internalized the lie of the criminal justice system: that Black and brown people are intrinsically bad and more deserving of incarceration than others. They believed that they deserved a plantation life.

It's easy to blame yourself for your pain, especially when all of society is feeding you the line. It's much harder to open to the possibility that you're in this painful and prolonged predicament simply because the world is unjust. Because the world is against you. Because the world is anti-Black and the very people who are paid to protect you are the ones who are shooting at you and stopping-and-frisking you and arresting you and charging you and imprisoning you. Where is the hope in that? Where is the Divine in that?

During my reflective walk, I was reminded of a story from Christian scripture in which Jesus makes one of his final statements before his crucifixion. In the traditional telling, Christ, while on the cross, engages in conversation with the two people who are also being crucified. One of the people (labeled a "criminal" in the Gospel of Luke) speaks to Christ on behalf of both people saying, *We are punished justly, for we are getting what our deeds deserve.* But [you have] done nothing wrong" (Luke 23:41; emphasis mine). In the course of the conversation, Christ absolves the "criminals" of their sins and promises them entrance into Heaven, declaring: "The truth is, today you'll be with me in paradise!" (Luke 23:43). Channeling the audacity of the Kongolese who believed Christ to be a female ancestor as well, I asked myself: What if I reimagined this story and instead of a white male jesus on the cross, I envisioned an enslaved Black female ancestor on the cross? In other words, what if Black Madonna were on the cross? What would she say to the "criminals" in this story? Immediately, the words "You're with me now, and I'm handling it" rose to the surface of my consciousness.

As a Black mother, Black Madonna can't look at this "criminal" without seeing the faces of her Black and brown family members: her nephews, nieces, and niblings, her siblings, her uncles and aunts, her grandbabies. As many of us know, to Black women, mass incarceration isn't an abstract sociological phenomenon. It's not cocktail-hour fodder that we use to impress our neoliberal colleagues. It's personal. It's our cousins, our siblings, our parents. It's us. I don't know one Black woman who isn't personally affected by the threat and reality of mass incarceration. As our ancestor, Black Madonna is no different. She knows exactly who is on the cross next to her. And as a victim of state-sanctioned violence herself, surely she sees that this "criminal" isn't a criminal at all. He's a beautiful Black boy whose joy has been extinguished by all the forces of his anti-Black society. Surely, she sees that he has believed the lie that society has fed him—the lie that he deserves to be up on that cross, that he deserves the worst of it. Surely, she knows that he is fettered to the plantation and in desperate need of affirmation, empowerment, and liberation.

Black Madonna says, *You're with me now. And I'm handling it.*

By inviting the Black man who has been branded a criminal into her paradise (Luke 23:43), she is restoring his identity, even as he is insisting upon his shame. Shame and self-blame isolate us, disconnecting us from the rich resources that abound in even the starkest places. But she is inviting him into her fellowship. In his moment of deepest pain, she is healing his shame through community. *You're with me now,* she says. *What society says about you isn't true. What society says about your worth isn't true. What society says about your body isn't true. What society says about your intelligence isn't true. What society says about your morality isn't true. Look beyond what you can physically see, and enter into my paradise and encounter your true self.* As artist Mark Steven Greenfield attests, "The Black Madonnas . . . serve as both witnesses and teachers."[13]

She is offering a way off the plantation. A way out of shame and self-blame. A new birth. A new identity. A new reality. As I continued walking on the wooded plantation, I came upon the ruins of a cabin that housed enslaved people. While standing there, I was powerfully reminded that Black Madonna, who empowered the Kongolese to set themselves free, knows all about the walls that have held us back and has even personally experienced them herself. Yet she makes all things new. As poet Cynthia Dewi Oka says, "The revolution is not about self-defense. It's about self-creation, it's about seeing farther than the walls directly in front of us."[14] As I sat among the ruins and considered the diverse stories of Black Madonna that I have collected or encountered in books, I realized that across history and the African diaspora, Black Madonna is busting through the plantation walls so that all people of African descent can get a glimpse of what's beyond, a glimpse of our true selves, our postcolonial selves. But the first person through the wall always gets bloody. Always. And Black Madonna's willing to be that person. She's handling it. She's beckoning us all toward her so we may be fully free and return to help others get fully free.

A BLACK MADONNAISSANCE

As Black people who live in a society in which Black women are six times more likely to be killed than white women; the chains of slavery still exist in the form of mass incarceration; Black LGBTQIA people continue to experience rampant shaming and marginalization in Black church spaces; the school-to-prison pipeline insists on viewing Black children as threats; and Black justice advocates are constantly facing exhaustion, disillusionment, and burnout—we're *all* too sacred for this. As we continue to liberate ourselves and our communities, we need a robust spiritual resource who has reliably guided and nourished our ancestors for millennia.

As I hope to show you throughout this book, Black Madonna is precisely the spiritual resource we need for such a time as this. Black Madonna is multifaceted: an icon of resistance, a mother of abundance, and a nourisher of souls. As I have encountered hundreds of stories across eras, religions, and continents about how people have experienced Black Madonna, the most common thread I find is empowerment and accompaniment. Her ability to heal, transform, and embolden people is unfathomable; there's a reason why the Black Madonna of Montserrat in northern Spain is the second-most visited pilgrimage shrine *in the history of Christianity*. Further, as a cosmic mother, she never turns away an opportunity to affirm, heal, and support her children.

She's the one you call when the situation is especially dire and messy.

She's the one you call just after you experience a devastating and unfathomable loss and you don't even have the words so you just wail because you can trust that she gets it.

She's the one you call when the colonial programming has hacked away at you and you need a fortifying and fierce reminder that you are sacred, you are enough just as you are, and you are fully beloved.

She's the one you call when society has gaslit you so much that you can't even hear your own truth anymore.

She's the one you call when all you know is captivity and you need a North Star that can guide you off the plantation and into true freedom.

She's the one you call when the institutional church has programmed you to be exclusively subservient and submissive and you can't even imagine another way of being.

She's the one you call when the systems of oppression are befuddling and you need a cosmic resource who can help you "make a way out of no way" forward.

She's the one you call when you're drowning in shame and need someone to breathe life and liberation into your identity.

She's the one you call when the clamor of resource scarcity is drowning out the cheer of abundance.

She's the one you call when colonialism has plucked you from your African roots and you need an accessible pathway back into your diasporic family.

She's the one you call when you need a God who is unwaveringly and unquestionably on the side of the oppressed.

She's the one you call when you need a spirituality that can affirm the sacredness of Black trans people.

She's the one you call when you're facing a seemingly impossible situation and you need someone you trust to handle it.

She's the one you call when you realize you're simply too sacred for this.

While we continue to break free from the plantations that litter our social and spiritual landscape, navigate an increasingly cunning system of oppression, and weave pathways to hope and holistic wellness for *all* Black people, Black Madonna stands as a unifying divine being who brings all the children of the African diaspora into life and liberation. She harkens us back to a holistic spirituality that is rooted in the divine feminine and is thus deeply relational, and that predates the plantation and is thus free of colonial entrapments.

To all who want to be fully free and help others get fully free: It's time we follow in the footsteps of our ancestors and call our Cosmic Momma. And as we'll soon discover, she's been answering our call since the beginning of time.

We just didn't know it.

NICKNAMING OUR MOMMA

During my first Black Madonna pilgrimage, in which I visited 18 Black Madonnas in the Auvergne region of France, I found myself falling into the practice of giving each Black Madonna a nickname. I wasn't sure if I was being heretical, or disrespectful, but after I made a personal connection with a Black Madonna, I couldn't help but nickname her. For example:

- The Black Madonna of Vichy is officially called Our Lady of the Sick, but I nicknamed her She Who Cherishes Our Hot Mess.

- The Black Madonna of Mayres is officially called Our Lady of the Rock, but I call her Our Lady of the Side-Eye.

- The Black Madonna of Mende is titled Our Lady of the Fountain, but I call her She Whose Thick Thighs Save Lives.

With each Black Madonna I visited, I allowed my *experience* with her to guide my nickname for her. Case in point: When I encountered Our Lady of the Side-Eye, whose shrine literally depicts her side-eyeing a white man, I *felt* her solidarity with Black women who have been side-eyeing white patriarchy since its inception. But I also allowed my *need* for Black Madonna's intervention to guide my nicknames. For example, as a recovering perfectionist, I really need Black Madonna to cherish my hot mess and liberate me from the false belief that I must clean myself up, "act right," and never make mistakes in order to receive divine love. So calling her She Who Cherishes My Hot Mess was a way for me to proclaim my ongoing need for her.

It wasn't until a few months after my first pilgrimage that I discovered that nicknaming Black Madonna is not something I made up; it's a major part of her spiritual lineage. Since people have been calling on her, people have been nicknaming her. Many major Black Madonna shrines list multiple titles because people across different eras have called her by different names, depending on their experience of her and need for her. For example, the Black Madonna of Costa Rica is called La Negrita (Dear Black One), Our Lady of the Angels, Queen of Costa Rica, Queen of Workers, and Queen of Peace—and those are just the official titles! If you talk to people in the streets, you'll encounter numerous nicknames. Clarissa Pinkola Estés traveled across Central America asking the people what they call Black

Madonna, and she collected dozens of nicknames. Here's a sampling: She Who Leans Over from the Sky to Protect the Crops, She Who Is the Colorer of Cloth so People on Earth Can Be Seen from Heaven, She Who Carries the Soul Across Fenced Frontiers, Mother Storyteller, First Instructor, and She Who Never Moves.[15]

So we can rest assured that Black Madonna is a momma who not only loves to be called on but also loves to be nicknamed! As a deeply relational being, she wants to know how we see her and what we need from her. She invites us to boldly call on her with a unique nickname that signals our connection to her.

The Kongolese insurrectionists called Black Madonna their "Ancestor." Harriet Tubman called the Divine "the North Star." It's worth noticing that both of these nicknames emboldened the people to embrace their intrinsic sacredness and courageously walk into freedom. Because Harriet called the Divine the North Star, she was able to trust that each next step would be divinely guided—no matter how dark, scary, or uncertain the situation. And because the Kongolese called Black Madonna their Ancestor, they were able to boldly claim their sacredness and resist the plantation lie that they deserved to be enslaved.

Our nicknames for Black Madonna are proclamations, prayers, and spells; they nurture our personal connection to her and help shift our reality. If I call her my Ancestor, then I am sacred. Period. If I call her my North Star, then I am guided. Period. If I call her She Who Cherishes My Hot Mess, then I am cherished. Period.

Black Madonna invites us to give her a nickname that helps us embody the freedom she so generously offers.

So let's take a moment to gently check in with ourselves and ask what's stirring in us as we encounter Black Madonna as a momma we can call on to lead us into deeper freedom.

1. Are there any resonant nicknames that quickly rise to the surface? If so, write them down. If not, that's completely okay; the next few questions may help you encounter a nickname that nurtures your embodied soul. You may want to journal, draw, move/dance, or put a hand on your heart as you lovingly inquire:

    a.   How do I want to be more free? How do I *need* to be more free to embody my inherent sacredness?

    b.   Now what do I need Black Madonna to be in order to boldly walk toward deeper freedom? Do I need her to be trustworthy like an immovable rock? Do I need her to be wise like an ancient, deep-rooted tree? Do I need her to be bold and bright like divine lightning? Do I need her to be a protector? Do I need her to deftly reweave me like a grandmother spider?

2.   After reflecting on these questions, set a timer for five minutes and write or draw any needs and new names that rise to the surface of your mind.

3.   Once you have your list, proclaim the names out loud and without judgment. Simply notice how your body responds to hearing them. Is it invigorated? Is it downregulated? Does it feel enveloped by a blanket? Do your shoulders feel relaxed?

4.   Circle or highlight the name or names that especially resonate with your body and your needs.

5.   Take a few moments to reflect on the name or names. Do you feel Black Madonna speaking to you through it? Do you feel empowered to claim it as one of your personal nicknames for Black Madonna?

2

INVOCATION

Sacred Black Feminine, you are the first dawn.
Black Madonna, your radiant darkness spawned the sun.
In birthing yourself, you set life in motion.
Your infinite Blackness shot seeds of every color,
Confirming that life in any hue comes from you.

Sacred Black Feminine, you are the first matriarch,
Black Madonna, the Mother of all Gods.
White jesus confines you to meek and mild mother,
But we instinctively know better. For our ancestors called you
The Container of the God Whom Nothing Can Contain
And they planted their memory of you in our DNA.

Sacred Black Feminine, you are our first mother.
Black Madonna, this world has estranged us,
Yet your faint voice echoes brighter as we awaken.
For we recognize that we first heard your song
While our souls were being formed in your womb.
And we remember that you have been calling us all along.

Sacred Black Feminine, you are the first night,
Black Madonna, our Mother Darkness.
When the fears of this age consume us,
When we lie in bed at night and fret fret fret,
Remind us that we are fully safe and surrounded.
For the darkness is not a what but a who.
Yes, the darkness is entirely you.

Chapter 2

SHE HAS LOVED US SINCE THE BEGINNING OF TIME

Awakening to Black Madonna as the World's Oldest Deity

The kid was in a frenzy, and I had no idea what had set him off. One moment my four-year-old adopted nephew, Malcolm, was sitting on the golden hardwood floor, blissfully zoom-zoom-zooming his red fire engine toy across the living room, and the next moment he inexplicably rose and began stomping around in search of who knows what. Frustrated, he began to howl, and tears streamed down his caramel-colored cheeks as he continued pacing furiously.

I adore all four of my adopted niblings, but I have a special connection to Malcolm because we share an early August birth date (he is exactly 40 years younger than me) and we both embody that legendary and often-dysregulating Leo fire. And like a true Leo, Malcolm's rage was not marked by hysterical screams and wails. Rather, it was soulful and dramatically moody, like the giant in the "Jack and the Beanstalk" folktale. As Malcolm pounded the perimeter of the living room, he might as well have been chanting, "Fee-fi-fo-fum."

Noticing his distress, his mother, my dear friend Leah, lovingly called out to him, "Malcolm, are you okay? It looks like you could use some help. Can Mommy help you? What do you need?"

Malcolm didn't verbally respond; instead he furiously shook his head and continued thrashing about the room.

Never one to abandon her child, Leah tried again. "Mommy would love to help you. What do you need? Do you need a snuggle? A snack? To go poo?"

Nothing, just more fee-fi-fo-fum vibes.

Supernaturally patient, Leah beseeched him yet again. "Okay, Malcolm, I can see you're working some things out, so I'm going to give you the space to do that. But I want you to know that whenever you're ready for help, I'm here. Mommy is willing to help you with whatever you need to feel at peace and get regulated."

Leah's final plea seemed to exacerbate Malcolm's inner Leo. *"I'm regulated! I'm regulated! I'm regulated! I'm regggggggggulaaaaaaaated,"* he roared as he continued stomping around the room.

A better auntie probably wouldn't have laughed, but I couldn't help but giggle at the sight of my adorable and completely dysregulated nephew claiming to be regulated. Malcolm was the embodiment of dysregulation, yet he refused to admit it and receive help from his compassionate and well-resourced mother. After running around the house for another 20 minutes, he ran out of stubborn energy and collapsed in Leah's loving arms. Finally able to receive his mother's care, he fell asleep on her breast, and the entire house exhaled into tranquility.

The giant was finally at peace.

THE MALCOLM IN ME

Later that day when I reflected on the incident, I smiled again but this time because I saw myself in Malcolm's obstinate dysregulation. For the past month, I had been completely dysregulated. My body full of capitalism-fueled anxiety, I couldn't find a way to quiet myself. As the cost of living in the U.S. waxed and support for Black activists and artists waned, every single cell in my body carried its own worry.

Will my racial justice leadership business survive now that DEI budgets have dried up?

Will I be able to pay my mortgage?

Will I be able to continue making monthly mutual aid contributions to the marginalized communities with whom I have relationships?

Does my offering to the world even matter if it is not valued by the capitalist marketplace?

Almost every night I awoke around 2 A.M., roused by the questions and my dwindling savings account.

Since I'm not a four-year-old, I didn't express my dysregulation by thrashing about the house. Instead, I expressed it by obsessively opening Instagram on my phone in the middle of the night and doom scrolling. I expressed it by neglecting my meditation practice in favor of bingeing yet another Netflix show. I expressed it by silencing my inner wisdom and allowing my fear to convince me to say yes to exploitative projects that promised to pay. I expressed it by judging the Black female small business owners who seemed to be thriving. *Oh she's just doing well because she's a sellout*, I would tell myself.

Sleeplessness. Compulsive behaviors. Overworking. Critical judgments.

Like Malcolm, I was giving fee-fi-fo-fum vibes.

My expressions of dysregulation temporarily muffled the anxiety, only for it to return louder and more voracious than ever. But as I reflected on the incident with Malcolm and Leah, I was reminded that, like Malcolm, I have a choice. I can either remain obstinate in my dysregulation, unwilling to admit it and carrying on alone, or I can tune in to Black Madonna, who, like Leah, is unwilling to abandon me no matter how dysregulated I become. But it's no surprise that I struggle to turn toward this wonderful and ever-present Black Madonna, who, frankly, seems too good to be true. My traumatized body and psyche are reluctant to trust that such an expansive and limitless love can exist. Like Malcolm, I hesitate to respond to Black Madonna's loving call.

Can I trust this God?

Can I be vulnerable with this God?

Can I bring my dysregulated self to this God?

Will she help me or will she recoil?

Even after years of intentionally awakening to Black Madonna and effortfully reorienting my identity and spirituality around her life-giving, unconditional love, I still hesitate to reach out to her when I am most desperate because the fearmongering and judgmental voice of the patriarchal god of my spiritual origins often colonizes my consciousness. When I am dysregulated and desperate, rather than spelunking my psyche for the deep truths about her limitless love, I revert to the old stories and beliefs that I was taught when I was a young girl.

A LIMITED LOVE

When I pause and reflect on my upbringing in our anti-nurturing, patriarchal society, I begin to understand why I'm skeptical of Black Madonna's unconditional love and reluctant to trust it. Black Madonna's love is such a stark contrast to the very limited love that my biological parents offered me. It's difficult to believe in, much less surrender to, a limitless love when your childhood experiences suggest that such a love does not exist. Unlike Black Madonna's expansive and unconditional love, patriarchy has taught us that love is a reward for good behavior, superior performance, and perfect alignment with other people's expectations of us. Even more so, patriarchy has taught us that love can easily be snatched away if we don't keep working hard to earn it.

Often, even the most well-meaning parents and caregivers were taught as children that love is limited and that perfection is the only pathway to love. Perhaps you can relate? For example, by the time I was Malcolm's age, I was painfully aware that parental love had conditions. A fastidious and perfectionistic child—whether it was cleaning my booty after a poop, helping paint my bedroom walls the color yellow, memorizing my lines in the annual Christmas pageant, or helping my mother with the household chores—I wanted everything to be *just right*. Most of the time, I met my own unrealistic standards, and when that happened, I was the apple of my father's eye and rewarded with loving praise. But when I failed, a violent hell was unleashed.

I must have been born with a sweet tooth, and back in the early '80s, my sugar-hungry taste buds were all about cherry-red Kool-Aid, which my mom often served at dinner. I was a typical four-year-old, so naturally I wanted to first fill up on the sugary drink, then gobble up my chicken, and then ignore the veggies and rice that remained on my plate. My young dad would often say, "Neena loves her meats and sweets."

Dad was right. I loved meats and sweets. I still do.

One night Dad instituted a new dinnertime rule: "No one is allowed to drink their Kool-Aid until they have finished eating their food."

I reluctantly but hurriedly consumed my veggies (my mom was on a zucchini kick at the time, and it was excruciating) and then moved on to my rice. All that remained was the good stuff: my chicken and Kool-Aid. Relieved, I took a swig of my Kool-Aid before taking a stab at the chicken.

You see, in my little four-year-old head, "meats and sweets" went together. It didn't occur to me that the chicken was "food" and that I had been instructed to eat it before I drank any Kool-Aid.

As soon as my dad witnessed my mistake, he grabbed me by the arm and dragged me to my parents' room, where I received a severe beating for being "willfully disobedient."

I remember trying to explain that I hadn't meant to disobey and that I had misunderstood the rule, but he was unable to hear my side of the story because he had already declared my story: that I was willfully disobedient. I think that my "imperfection" triggered fear in him, that he got scared when I did something different from what he thought he had asked me to do. The fear then descended into a shame spiral because how could he possibly be a good (patriarchal) father if he couldn't control his four-year-old? This is how patriarchal religion uses imperfection, missed connections, and maladaptive behavior to keep us under its control—by shaming us for our imperfection and convincing us that our imperfection says something about our lovability and core identity. It's a clever ploy. We can stay trapped in this cycle of alienation for a lifetime—perpetually afraid that our imperfection poisons our humanity and eager to earn "love" by striving to meet an impossible standard of perfection.

AN ALTAR TO A WILD PASSING GOD

Given my story, it's no wonder that Black Madonna's unconditional and expansive love often seems unfamiliar—or worse, untrustworthy. Those of us who have been conditioned to believe that we must earn love, or that we must always act a certain way in order to be worthy of love, are perfect candidates for Black Madonna's transformative and limitless love. She wants to heal the pain of our childhood experiences and show us what it feels like to receive unconditional love, especially in the midst of our "ugliest" moments. Black Madonna wants us to know that she adores the Malcolm within each of us. She assures us that our tantrums don't repel her or diminish her love for us. In fact, she loves to mother us and relishes the opportunity to help us find our grounding and peace in the midst of dysregulation.

Black Madonna's limitless love is beautifully embodied by author and lecturer Ijeoma "Ej" Clement-Akomolafe, who, according to her husband, philosopher Bayo Akomolafe, insists that they not call their young son's dysregulated behavior a *meltdown*.

"He's not having a meltdown," Ej declares. "He's creating an altar to a wild, passing God."[1]

Black Madonna's paradigm-shifting love invites us to rethink everything we think we know about perfection, "bad" behavior, tantrums, and meltdowns. Our dysregulated behavior isn't a problem or failure. Rather, it's an invitation to offer ourselves to a God who loves and embraces our wildness, a God who is not offended by us and doesn't need us to be anything other than our authentic selves. Our patriarchal, colonial society has invented judgmental terms like *meltdown*, *tantrum*, and *identity crisis* to shame us for simply needing help. More often than not, human parents tend to punish us for being dysregulated rather than guiding us, helping us, and reminding us that we are not alone in our distress. As children of a patriarchal and colonial society, we encounter hostile institutions in every corner of our lives: exacting grading systems in schools, punitive judicial systems, unforgiving credit scores, and legalistic and judgmental spiritual communities. Concepts like *sin* are often used to reaffirm our patriarchal religious conditioning, teaching us that it's not okay to make mistakes or need constructive feedback or loving correction. It's difficult to find communities in which our dysregulation is welcome and seen as a glorious marker of our humanity. It's no wonder that many of us believe that we must numb our dysregulation; for if we show it, we may be shamed and expelled.

But dysregulation is our body's way of alerting us to an ancient truth that colonialism and patriarchy have tried their darndest to extinguish: that since the dawn of humanity, people have been calling out to a wild, passing God. If we listen to our bodies, especially in the quiet of the night when our worries are screaming the loudest, we may hear the loving whisper of the prehistoric wild, passing God who is still wild and still circling us today. She is wild like a mother lion, yet imminently tender and protective. Rather than chastising us as our dysregulated bodies cry out to her, she embraces us.

Traversing the globe and history books in search of the mystical heart of Black Madonna, researcher Ean Begg has discovered a curious fact: Many ancient Black Madonnas are found near statues of lions and are associated with the mother lion. Begg writes that Black Madonna is a lioness, and lionesses "lick their cubs into shape and life."[2] Rather than chastising us, Black Madonna fiercely and lovingly beckons us to come near her so she can show us that we can let down our guard with her and she will not judge, punish, or spank us. Instead, she wants to lick, clean, groom, and care for us so much that we become mature, loving, and fierce lions too. When we surrender to her holy licks, we become people who live fully and without fear, no matter what is going on around us. Black Madonna the Lioness promises us that if we lean on her breast and allow our cheek to rest on hers, we will become whole.

Black Madonna embodies the liberating truth that Clarissa Pinkola Estés beautifully articulates: "Sorrow and sin are not curses, not referendums presuming a defect of a soul. They are instead signals that a soul is hurting and needs lifting up, re-arighting. They mean this soul who came to these injuries in whatever way, is in need of care, cleansing, and aid. By way of simple sacred rite, and most of all in loving reassertion of the consciousness with 'Source without source,' the soul is reset like a jewel into center again."[3]

If you're anything like me, this wild, passing lioness God might seem unfamiliar and even perhaps suspicious. If you've never been introduced to Black Madonna the Lioness, how can you trust her enough to receive her loving licks? Like me, you may be asking yourself:

Can I trust this God?

Can I be vulnerable with this God?

Can I bring my dysregulated self to this God?

And will she help me or will she recoil?

If these questions resonate with you, you are not alone. For we will soon discover that the affirmative answer to all these questions lies in the oldest deity known to humankind, which I call "the Sacred Black Feminine." Since the dawn of humanity, people have instinctively known that a loving and powerful Sacred Black Feminine presides over all of creation. Over the millennia, as empires have risen, colonialism has infected the globe, and hierarchy has replaced communal living, we have lost our collective connection to the Sacred Black Feminine of prehistoric sub-Saharan Africa. Our dysregulated bodies are calling out for her, but we are such a long way from her and the land in which we first experienced her that we cannot see that she is still lovingly circling us.

THE OG GOD

Though many of us are just discovering her now, Black Madonna has always been present. She has always been our Mother Lioness. She has always been at our side. She has always nourished and protected us. In fact, she is the oldest deity the world has ever known. Consider this: Before patriarchal religion, there was Black Madonna. Before YHWH, the Jewish and Christian God, there was Black Madonna. Before Muhammad and the Buddha, there was Black Madonna. Before Jesus Christ, there was Black Madonna. Archaeology and genetics research have confirmed what the famed psychoanalyst Carl Jung instinctively knew to be true: that the world's oldest and most enduring sacred archetype is that of a prehistoric Black female deity.[4]

In our contemporary society with its dominant white patriarchal god, it seems almost unfathomable that for most of human history, people worshipped the Sacred Black Feminine. But when we go off colonial autopilot and stop to think about it, it makes sense. Many of us are aware that, in a sense, we are all Africans. Geneticists have tracked the DNA of populations around the globe and confirmed that the origins of all humans go back to sub-Saharan Africa, to the several "Eves" (e.g., first women) of Africa around 50,000 BCE. But what is less known is that the original deity of our prehistoric African ancestors was not white or male. Since at least the 1970s, archaeologists such as Emmanuel Anati have uncovered compelling historical evidence confirming that the oldest divinity in human history is Black and female—the Sacred Black Feminine, a prehistoric version of our beloved Black Madonna.

The early humans believed that the Sacred Black Feminine was the sole source of life, the primordial darkness that existed before anything else and contained within it all that the universe would eventually become. According to professor Sheri Parks, "She was everything, the original complete being. She symbolized the power of the forces that ultimately shaped all of life and death, of space, time, and matter. She was pregnant . . . and when She gave birth, having lain with no one, the world as we know it began."[5]

The Sacred Black Feminine was not some B-level god, like a second-tier superhero in the Marvel Universe. As the Supreme Being, she was universally revered as a vast and formidable force who facilitated the cycle of birth, death, and rebirth—both in humans and in nature. As the Great Mother, she was the egg, the sperm, the womb, *and* the midwife of all living things. "She was the Mother of All, the mother of life itself and of every form that eventually arose—the heavens, the earth, the underworld, the gods, the good and the evil, the dark and the light, the beautiful and the horrible."[6] One ancient text surveyed the Sacred Black Feminine's expansive qualities, listing them for all to hear. She was "intelligent, holy, unique, manifold, subtle, mobile, incisive, unsullied, lucid, invulnerable, benevolent, shrewd, irresistible, beneficent, friendly to human beings, steadfast, dependable, unperturbed, almighty, [and] all-surveying . . ."[7]

Our ancient ancestors were well acquainted with the Sacred Black Feminine's astonishing complexity and power and duly gave her illustrious and majestic names such as Queen of Heaven, Lady of the High Place, Celestial Ruler, Lady of the Universe, Sovereign of the Heavens, Lioness of the Sacred Assembly,[8] and Divine Ancestress.[9]

But as both "the womb and the tomb of the world," the Sacred Black Feminine was also intimately involved in the people's lives. During the most tender of human moments—the joy and agony of birth and the pain and peace of death—the Sacred Black Feminine held the people closely. Because she was involved in their everyday rhythms, such as planting and harvesting, and birthing and dying, the people knew that she was a deeply relational deity and that they could call on her when in need. Though the Sacred Black Feminine was formidable, Parks asserts that even her "rage was compassionate."[10]

Despite all the ways that patriarchy has tried to erase our human memory of the Sacred Black Feminine and extinguish our connection to her, she remains alive and *with* us and *for* us. In fact, she has traveled across time and space in order to pursue us and show us that she has not and will not ever abandon us.

One of the most defining aspects of the Sacred Black Feminine is that she does not abandon her children. Period. Where her people go, she goes and makes her loving presence known to them. In her epic book *Dark Mother: African Origins and Godmothers*, Lucia Chiavola Birnbaum traces the Sacred Black Feminine's journeys across eras and continents in order to stick by her people's side.[11] When the earliest sub-Saharan African humans migrated north and west into the regions that we now call northern Africa, southwest Asia, Asia, and the Americas, the Sacred Black Feminine followed them, her image captured in the form of prehistoric statues and symbols that still exist in local caves and crypts. As her people settled into each new locale, she revealed herself in a way that was culturally resonant and assured them of her presence. For example, in northern Africa, she revealed herself as the Egyptian supergoddess Isis; in southwest Asia she embraced her people as the Mesopotamian supergoddess Inanna; in Asia, she embodied the Hindu supergoddess Kali and the Buddhist supergoddess Tara; and, in South America, she manifested as the Incan supergoddess Pachamama. Though her religious affiliation and some cultural markers shifted along with each migration, her Blackness and femininity remained constant, as did her powerful love for her people and her core characteristics as creatrix and holder of life and death, overseer of planting and harvesting, throne of wisdom, supreme queen, and fierce protector.

In late antiquity as Canaanite traders from southwest Asia migrated to Europe, the Sacred Black Feminine followed them in their devotion to Isis and new-to-the-scene Black female deities such as Black Artemis of Ephesus and Cybele of Phrygia. Eventually the Roman Empire expanded, and patriarchal Christianity, terrified of all these powerful female deities, outlawed any worship of them—and in some cases even violently demolished existing temples and built Catholic churches on the same sites. During this time, the Sacred Black Feminine largely went underground, disguising herself in the icons of Black Madonna.

To be certain, the people knew that when they encountered and prayed to a Black Madonna icon, they were not praying to the white, porcelain-skinned, disempowered Virgin Mary who had been strategically sidelined as the Mother of God (as opposed to God herself). They knew that the weak and white Virgin Mary was a figment of the patriarchal Christian imagination and was not to be confused with the powerful Black Madonna their ancestors worshipped as the Sacred Black Feminine.

Beneath the Catholic trappings, they instinctively knew that Black Madonna was no weak-willed and powerless handmaiden of a male God. Rather, she was God herself, their beloved Sacred Black Feminine, who remained with them through thick and thin. In this way, the people were able to carry on their worship of the Sacred Black Feminine right under the Catholic Church's nose.

In a violently hierarchical and inequitable serfdom that was essentially powered by the Catholic Church, the people knew they couldn't turn to white Mary, the subservient feminine mascot of the Church, for empowerment and protection. They knew that only their fierce and formidable Sacred Black Feminine—whom they once knew as Isis, Artemis, and Cybele but now called Black Madonna—would come to their aid. Painfully aware that they couldn't call on the white Mary at their local Catholic parish, medieval pilgrims often traversed harsh mountain ranges, crossed harrowing war zones, and expended significant resources on pilgrimages to the famous Black Madonnas of Rocamadour (France), Montserrat (Spain), and Montevergine (Italy) to ask for help.

In this way, the Black Madonnas stood out among the Marian shrines and became major pilgrimage destinations. As I mentioned in Chapter 1, the Black Madonna of Montserrat is the second-most frequented pilgrimage site *in the history of Christianity*, second only to the Camino de Santiago pilgrimage route (which, not surprisingly, is home to numerous Black Madonna shrines). Further, many Black Madonnas, such as the Black Madonna of Toulouse (France), were nicknamed "the Black One" in part so that desperate pilgrims clearly understood which Mary to pray to; since many Catholic churches contain multiple images and statues of Mary, they didn't want to make the mistake of praying to the wrong Mary, the white Mary. In times of great need, pilgrims made sure to look for the Black One, for she was the one they could count on. Even today, Black Madonna shrines, which make up a fraction of the Marian shrines in the world, are among the most visited—such as the Black Madonna of Częstochowa (Poland), who welcomes over 5 million visitors per year. Much like our medieval counterparts, contemporary spiritual seekers know that when we really need help, we'd better call Black Madonna.

FEE-FI-FO-SNOOZE

Trapped in my Malcolm-like dysregulation and after weeks of sleepless, middle-of-the-night doomscrolling on social media, I decided to call Black Madonna. That evening when I went to bed, I placed a small statue of Black Madonna directly on top of my phone, which lay on my bedside table. That way, when I awoke in the night and compulsively reached for my phone, I would grab the statue instead. In my groggy dysregulation, I wanted to train myself to reach for Momma.

Over the years I have collected dozens of antique Black Madonna statues. Most of them are battered and well loved and were found at French flea markets. For reasons that we'll explore in Chapter 5, many Black Madonnas in France are known for their power and wisdom, so most of the statues in my home exude those qualities. Standing or sitting tall, these French Black Madonnas are majestic and lovingly fierce. When I need to be reminded of Momma's ability to drop jaws, work miracles, and make shit happen, I turn to them. But during my most recent pilgrimage to France, I found a Black Madonna that offers a different invitation—one of nearness, intimacy, and tenderness. She's the kind of Black Madonna who seeks us out precisely when we're in the middle of a meltdown. In fact, this Black Madonna, who is called Our Lady of the Port, is a member of a rare class of Black Madonnas called "Virgins of Tenderness." Rather than holding the child on their lap or hoisted on their hip, Virgins of Tenderness nestle the child close to their body, in the curve of the neck. Our Lady of the Port embraces the child with such immense love and intimacy that even their cheeks touch.

I found my nine-inch metal statue of Our Lady of the Port at the bottom of a flea market bargain bin. She only cost me five euros, but the theological truth she emanates is priceless: that we are held, cherished, protected, and truly one with her. Her protective, cheek-to-cheek connection with her child promises us that nothing—not fear, not resource scarcity, not even air—separates us, her children, from her.

As I gazed at my little statue of Our Lady of the Port, I implicitly understood that she's most eager to embrace her children in the midst of our fee-fi-fo-fum moments. Never one to banish her children, Black Madonna calls out to her dysregulated children and says, "It looks like you could use some help. Can Momma help you? What do you need? Do you need a snack? A snuggle? To go poo?" In other words, do you need some nourishing wisdom? A visceral reminder that you are dearly loved? A chance to release burdens you were never meant to carry and discharge the false beliefs and toxic emotions that do not serve you?

Since many of us are plagued by shame and a lack of belonging, we often think that we are a nuisance to Black Madonna. But that couldn't be further from the truth. She cheers when we bring our dysregulated selves to her wild and welcoming altar. No matter how white patriarchy has shaped us, whatever is troubling us, whatever we are holding on to, whatever conundrum we think we must handle on our own—we can give it *all* to her. Our Lady of the Port powerfully illustrates the love the Hebrew psalmist longed for: "Let your arms wrap close around me [so] that I may remember that I am yours, flesh of your flesh."[12] It is precisely when we feel most lost, most unlovable, and least in control that we need to be reminded that we are not alone, that we are, in fact, hers. And as hers, we are unconditionally cherished, protected, and wanted.

But in a competitive and anti-nurturing world, it's so easy to forget that we are hers.

When the clamor of hierarchy, fear, and resource scarcity drowns out the gentle whisper of her love, the truth feels unreachable and distant. So I decided to write a short meditation to help rewire my relationship to Black Madonna when I'm trapped in dysregulating fear:

I belong to Momma.

I am fiercely loved.

I will never be abandoned.

I can surrender to her abundant care.

I committed the meditation to memory and resolved to repeatedly return to it whenever I needed a reminder of the truth. Practices like this are simple but powerful because they call up the ancient but forgotten truths that are buried deep within us. As Carl Jung asserted, the Sacred Black Feminine is such a primal archetype that we have inherited her into our collective unconscious. Whether we can easily and consciously access her or not, she is hardwired into our brain chemistry.[13] Practices like this help us consciously nurture our connection to the Sacred Black Feminine, who has been lovingly pursuing us since the beginning of time.

The night I wrote this meditation I placed my statue of Our Lady of the Port on top of my phone and went to bed with the meditation in my heart. Sure enough, when I awoke in the dark and groggily reached for my phone, I encountered the statue of Black Madonna. As soon as my fumbling and fearful fingers made contact with her cold, metal body, my spirit awakened and I recited and remembered her truth.

Caressing the statue, I felt the child peacefully leaning on Black Madonna's breast and was reminded that I could do the same.

I belong to Momma.

I am fiercely loved.

Rather than holding on to my worry, I took a deep breath, relaxed my body into her body, and gave my worry to her.

I will never be abandoned.

I can surrender to her abundant care.

Within a few moments, I fell back to sleep.

I continued this practice every night for weeks until my waking hours were no longer plagued by fear, insecurity, and abandonment and I was able to peacefully sleep through the night. Through this simple practice, the Black Madonna of the Port opened her eternal portal to me and showed me that since the beginning of time, she has loved, embraced, and claimed me as her own.

She has loved you since the beginning of time too, beloved.

Across history and around the globe, the Sacred Black Feminine has fiercely accompanied her people, ever reminding them that she has not forsaken them and that nothing, absolutely nothing, will separate them from her love, protection, and embrace. A deeply relational and loyal deity, she will morph, adapt, and even disguise herself in order to stick with us and care for us. But perhaps no Black Madonna better exemplifies the Sacred Black Feminine's fierce and loving pursuit of us than Our Lady of Charity, the Black Madonna of Cuba. Like many of the Afro-Cubans who venerate her, her story begins in central West Africa, where we will begin our exploration.

REWIRING OUR RELATIONSHIP TO THE DIVINE

The Black Madonna of the Port's cosmic tenderness dispels everything white patriarchy has conditioned us to believe about the Divine. She's a mother who loves to be close to us, loves to mother us, loves to teach us and be patient with us. No matter how many times we call out to her or how many times we need to learn a lesson the hard way, she never sighs with fatigue or annoyance when we call on her to guide us, remind us, and help us.

Nevertheless, our deeply ingrained white patriarchal spiritual DNA continues to interfere with our relationship with her. As we explored in this chapter, when we are distracted or in flight-or-flight mode, or in the middle of the night when consciousness is limited and fear is loud, we can easily forget that Black Madonna is with us and has been here all along, simply waiting for us to turn to her. This forgetting is so prevalent that I have a name for it; I call it being knocked off our "truth-roots." In other words, truths such as *we are unconditionally loved by Black Madonna and we are her precious children*, are powerful roots that steady, nourish, and empower us. But life's challenges and our patriarchal conditioning often threaten to disconnect us from these truths. Thankfully, with practice and intention, we can begin to rewire our spiritual DNA and form stronger pathways of connection to our truth-roots, the profound truths about *who* we are and *whose* we are.

Let's take a few minutes to create a personalized Black Madonna mantra, a simple, four-line truth nugget that we can readily use whenever we get knocked off our truth-roots and need a reminder. Written from the heart and with vulnerability, these are prayers or spells that can realign us within moments.

1. To begin, identify and list up to four stubborn lies about yourself and/or the world that continue to bug or even terrorize you. Oftentimes, these are lies that are based in real pain or trauma.

   For example, I experienced quite a bit of housing and financial insecurity when I was a child. So even though I'm not imminently at risk of homelessness, even a whiff of financial insecurity can knock me off my truth-roots and send me tumbling down a catastrophizing spiral that has me homeless in less than 72 hours. When I'm caught in the lie, I need Black Madonna to continue showing me that she is resourcing me and will keep a roof over my head.

You could also explore the nicknames you gave Black Madonna in the practice in Chapter 1 and expand on the stories behind them. For instance, if your nickname for Black Madonna is Compassionate Healer, consider what aspects of your story might have nurtured lies about the Divine's desire or ability to heal you and your community.

Example Lie 1: If I make one financial mistake or have one setback, I will lose my housing and no one will help me.

Example Lie 2: I shouldn't bother the Divine about my chronic pain.

2. Once you have listed up to four lies, write one short proclamation that corresponds to and refutes each lie. If you feel stuck on your proclamations, don't worry. That's what community is for—feel free to reach out to a beloved and ask them to co-imagine the truth nuggets that Black Madonna longs to give to you.

Example Proclamation 1: There is nothing I can do to lose Black Madonna's presence, support, and abundance in my life.

Example Proclamation 2: Black Madonna delights in hearing from me and welcomes all my thoughts, feelings, and needs.

3. Once you've identified your proclamations, make a list. If memorization is accessible to you and life-giving for you, I encourage you to memorize the list. However, writing or printing the list on a small piece of paper and carrying it in your tote, wallet, or back pocket is also a wonderful way to keep your truth nuggets handy and ready to support you right when you need them.

3
INVOCATION

Sacred Black Feminine, Mother of Limitless Love,
You follow us more intimately than our own shadows,
Ever reminding us that we are your first love,
Beloved children birthed in the primordial darkness.
Ancient Huntress, Diasporic Tracker,
We are marked by your love and claimed by you.
When forced migration disrupts our holy union—
Time and time again you traverse land and sea
To prove that you will never let us go.

Ọṣun, River Orisha, Mother of Limitless Love,
We bear your skin, dark and luscious like yours,
Ever affirming we are loved, your kin.
Shape-Shifting Spirit, Magical Momma,
Not abduction, nor slavery, nor mixing of race
Can exclude us from your sweetwater embrace.
When we were ripped from your river,
stolen far across the Atlantic,
You abandoned your home,
Became the rain that pursued us.
When colonizers diluted our African bloodlines
And lightened our skin, inherited from you—
Without hesitation you lightened your skin too,
Ever affirming we are loved, your kin.

Black Madonna, Our Lady of Charity,
    Mother of Limitless Love,
You left West Africa as Ọṣun and arrived in Cuba as Mary.
Proving again and yet again that no place
In your diaspora lies beyond your boundless space.
Cosmic Double Agent, Siren of Subterfuge,
You donned a disguise and clothed yourself in Catholicism,
so we could receive your love without raising suspicion.
A continent away from your native river,
you put down roots among your people in Cuba.
You crossed an ocean to accompany, empower, liberate.
To prove that no matter what they dictate,
Your home is with us and our home is in you.

Chapter 3

SHE CROSSES OCEANS FOR US

Receiving Black Madonna's Limitless Embrace

I recently pilgrimaged to the Black Madonnas of southern Italy with Alessandra Belloni, an elder Black Madonna teacher who exudes a holy mix of wisdom and eccentricity. The only African American in the pilgrimage group, I was surrounded by Italian Americans who could trace their ancestry to southern Italy and were eager to reconnect with their cultural and spiritual roots under Alessandra's loving guidance.

I wish I could have done the same.

As an African American whose beloved ancestors were forcibly trafficked to the United States over seven generations ago, I long to reclaim my true ancestral African roots. Many white Americans, like the others on the Italy pilgrimage, can track their ancestry by researching records at Ellis Island and other places where immigrant communities entered the U.S. For example, one of my Italian American friends knows precisely when his ancestors arrived here and even knows the exact names and locations of the obscure Italian villages from which they emigrated. But even if your privilege doesn't afford you that level of precision, many Americans can pinpoint the country from which their ancestors hailed.

But since my ancestors were not considered real humans, no records of their precolonial existence were maintained. Ever since I was a little girl growing up in the diverse San Francisco Bay Area, surrounded by Mexican, Filipino, white, and Indian neighborhood kids, I have felt a persistent hunger to connect with and reclaim my own ethnic roots. As an '80s kid, I had to rely on *The Cosby Show* and the miniseries *Roots* as I pieced together what it meant to be African American. That never really quite cut it, for we are ancient beings, and we are meant to root ourselves in our illustrious and expansive diasporic story. My story was both vague and only about 200 years old, and even as a kid I implicitly understood how impoverished it was.

I know I am not alone. For example, celebrated poet Nayyirah Waheed's words resonate deeply with many African Americans because she gives voice to the ancestral orphanhood that many of us experience. In one particularly evocative poem, "African American II" from her book *Salt,* Waheed describes the agony that many of us bear. As we awaken to our African lineage and begin to seek a connection, we must grapple with how culturally, linguistically, spiritually, and geographically alienated we are. Even if we hear Mother Africa calling to us from across the ocean, our vast estrangement hinders our ability to truly respond. In one gut-wrenching line Waheed illuminates this tragic reality: "i do not know how to say hello to my mother."[1]

As I grew into adulthood and intentionally nourished my Black identity, I began to understand my motherwound—my estrangement from my motherland as well as the far-reaching and sorrowful implications of that estrangement on my identity, spirituality, and sense of belonging in the world. Since my recorded ethnic lineage begins on the plantation, I lamented that my ethnic identity seemed born on the plantation. I longed to know who my people were before they became enslaved. I wanted to discover their stories, their songs, their languages, and their gods—and in doing so, discover more about my own identity and place in this world. And since my recorded spiritual lineage is tethered to the plantation, I lamented the ways that colonialism's white male Christ stripped me of a deeper, more embodied, Mother-centered Indigenous spirituality. Like Waheed, my heart was broken over the reality that I do not know how to greet my own Mother.

Though I remain heartbroken over the ways in which colonialism has trampled on my ethnic identity and stolen from my spiritual story, I am beginning to understand that, thanks to our beloved Black Madonna, I can learn to say hello to my Mother without knowing exactly where I am from. For as we explored in Chapter 2, Black Madonna is a contemporary portal to the ancient Sacred Black Feminine, who has revealed herself in just about every culture and era. Through Black Madonna, we are connected to all iterations of the Sacred Black Feminine. In fact, shortly after I awakened to Black Madonna, I learned that she is fully present in many Indigenous religions of the African diaspora—including Yoruba and Vodun in West Africa, Candomblé in Brazil, Voodoo in Haiti, and Santería in Cuba. For African Americans with Christian roots, Black Madonna is the perfect portal to our diasporic spiritual origins. As a Christian icon, Black Madonna is somewhat familiar and "speaks our spiritual language." Yet at the same time, her involvement in the diasporic religions broadens our spiritual horizons and invites us to reweave the spiritual tapestry that colonialism has torn apart.

In short, Black Madonna is the translator who helps us say hello to our ancestral Mother. When we examine Black Madonna's diasporic connections, we begin to understand that she has the power to heal our motherwound by showing us that there is no place in her diaspora that is beyond her reach and there is no person in her diaspora that is excluded from her embrace.

BLACK MADONNA'S DIASPORIC JOURNEY FROM NIGERIA TO CUBA

After tens of thousands of years of lovingly following her people everywhere they went and generously transforming into culturally relevant goddesses, the Sacred Black Feminine revealed herself to the Yoruba people of central West Africa, a people who practiced a rich and intricate polytheistic religion of numerous deities, spirits, and ancestors. Ever earnest to connect with her people in the deepest and most resonant way, the Sacred Black Feminine manifested in several of the orishas (divine spirits) of the Yoruba pantheon—including Yemọja, the oldest orisha, who was called "the mother of all orishas" and known to dwell in the ocean, and Ọṣun, the youngest orisha, who was known to dwell in the Ọṣun River in Nigeria. Rivers are a wonderful metaphor for the Sacred Black Feminine because they offer both practical and pleasurable gifts. For example, rivers offer water, transportation pathways for fish, natural irrigation, and food, among other things. But rivers supply their practical gifts with pleasurable flair—alongside the soothing sound of rushing water, among astonishing waterfalls, and with the pitch-perfect cooling sensation when you dip your sweaty toes in fresh water on a hot day. Rivers don't just deliver life; they deliver *abundant* life!

Like a river, Ọṣun offers both practical gifts and astonishing beauty and tranquility. In addition to being known for providing for the practical needs of her people, Ọṣun is also the orisha of love, pleasure, sensuality, and prosperity. Like her people, Ọṣun has gorgeous dark skin that has been kissed by the sun a thousand times. Additionally, she is often depicted as a voluptuous woman clothed in golden garments, resting under the abundant shade of a riverside tree and enjoying a delicious pot of exquisitely sweet honey. Her image alone invites her devotees to savor the sweetness of life, even when life is challenging. Ọṣun is all about that abundant life, and she doesn't just want her people to survive; she wants them to thrive!

So imagine Ọṣun's deep sorrow when European colonizers began to systematically abduct her beloved Yoruba people and traffic them across the Atlantic Ocean. As a 16th-century iteration of the Sacred Black Feminine, Ọṣun desperately longed to follow her people. As Yoruba scholar Ócha'ni Lele explains, many of the orishas were secreted in the bellies or hair of their priests and thus accompanied their devotees to foreign lands.[2] But as a river orisha who lived in the sweet waters of Nigeria, Ọṣun could only follow her people as far as where the river meets the sea. Once the fresh waters became salty, Ọṣun could not travel any further. Desperate to be reunited with her people, Ọṣun went to her powerful big sister Yemọja for help.

As tears of sadness and anger flowed from Ọṣun's eyes, she queried, "Sister, where did my people go? What is their life like now? How can I be reunited with them so I can provide for them and offer them abundant life?"

Though Yemọja was also a 16th-century archetype of the Sacred Black Feminine, as the oldest orisha and the mother of all orishas, she was more powerful than her little sister, Ọṣun. Further, as the ocean orisha, she had the capacity to follow her devotees across the saltwater seas.

"Sister," said Yemọja, "our people are being stolen away to a place called Cuba, and those of us who are able are going with them in spirit to watch over them, to protect them as best as we can."[3]

Then Yemọja began to tell Ọṣun about the horrifying treatment the Yoruba people were experiencing in Cuba. In just a few short years, the enslaved Yoruba people had been violently stripped of the markers and rituals that fostered their connection to Ọṣun and forced to assimilate into Spanish-Cuban society. Their skin, once dark and kissed by the African sun, became lighter and lighter as they sometimes voluntarily but often involuntarily procreated with Indigenous people and Spanish whites. Their illustrious Yoruba surnames were replaced by Spanish names. According to historian María Elena Díaz, their abundant spirituality, once tethered to the African land and rivers and rooted in African sacred rituals, was ripped away from them, and they were forced into Christian baptism.[4] Through the brutal and swift process of colonial disbursement, the Yoruba people were robbed of the names, rituals, land, and skin color that once directly connected them to the Sacred Black Feminine through the archetype of Ọṣun. Cosmic orphans without protection or provision, many of the people were conditioned to believe that Ọṣun had abandoned them and that their racial mixing and colonial estrangement had erased their sacredness and forever banished them to the lonely land of unbelonging.

Unwilling to abandon her people, Ọṣun begged Yemọja to help her cross the vast ocean. Yemọja happily complied by miraculously transforming Ọṣun into the rain so that she could travel in fresh water across the saltwater seas and be reunited with her people. As the deeply relational orisha of love, Ọṣun was supremely invested in their knowing that she would accompany them, no matter how far colonialism took them.

But the stunningly beautiful Ọṣun had one special request: Since many of her people were now multiracial and thus light-skinned, she asked Yemọja to lighten her dark skin to a creamy caramel color. She didn't do this in order to meet the European colonial standard of beauty. As the orisha of beauty, it was Ọṣun who set the standard, not colonialism. Rather, Ọṣun was concerned that after years of oppression and estrangement from her, her people had lost touch with their beauty and their belovedness to her. She became caramel colored so that they could see themselves in her and know with certainty that they too were beautiful. Ọṣun became caramel colored so that her orphan-hearted people would be assured that they belonged to her.

Unwilling to let her Black and brown people believe that they were forgotten, forsaken, and unprotected, Ọṣun pledged to vacate her sacred river lands, cross an ocean, and undergo a series of transformations from a dark-skinned river goddess to raindrops to a caramel-colored divine being—all in the service of love. In doing so, Ọṣun powerfully demonstrated the way that, time and again, the Sacred Black Feminine expresses her undying love for us.

ỌṢUN AND BLACK MADONNA: TWO SIDES OF THE SAME COIN

Around 1604, less than one full generation into the Cuban colonial period, Ọṣun carried out her mission, transforming into rain and crossing the Atlantic Ocean in a storm. As the sun rose and the raging seas settled, she transfigured into a small, caramel-colored statue of the Virgin Mary and bobbed on the surface of the water in the Bay of Nipe near El Cobre, a small copper mining village not far from the coast that was primarily populated by royal enslaved people who worked in the king of Spain's copper mines. Three enslaved boys—a ten-year-old, caramel-colored, multiracial boy named Juan Moreno and two Indigenous brothers named Juan and Rodrigo de Hoyos— happened to be canoeing toward some salt mines in the Bay of Nipe and were the first to encounter her when she appeared.[5] At first, the boys thought that they had spotted a bird amid the foamy sea. But as they drew near, they discovered an image of the Virgin Mary bearing an engraved sign that said, "I am the Virgin of Charity."[6] Consistent with her trademark fabulousness, Ọṣun's appearance itself contained a miracle: Juan Moreno ecstatically reported that although Ọṣun rose from the sea, her clothes were immaculately dry!

Ọṣun's commitment to love and care for her people was so great that she transformed into rain and crossed a vast ocean just to be with them and reclaim them as her own. Ọṣun's commitment to assuring her people that they were irrevocably beloved and beautiful was so deep that she was willing to radically change her own appearance in order to mirror theirs. This level of commitment is typical for the Sacred Black Feminine. For millennia, the Sacred Black Feminine has been pursuing humans with a profound and limitless love. Drawing from her inherent wisdom and vast experience, she knows exactly what it means to embody and communicate a profound and eternal love. Her love isn't a fickle love, nor is it shortsighted. She doesn't cross oceans like a passionate but immature lover who brashly proclaims their love but is clueless when it comes to embodying it. On the contrary, as an ancient being who understands humans better than we understand ourselves, the Sacred Black Feminine has forever known what clinical psychology research has just recently revealed to humans: that love is most effective when it is communicated in a way that makes sense to the recipient. In other words, profound love doesn't play games, keep the recipient guessing, or even require the recipient to decipher its meaning. Profound love speaks directly to the recipient's deepest and even unconscious stories, affirming that they are cherished, embraced, protected, seen, and irreplaceable. Practically speaking, profound love is freely given and ever willing to go the distance in order to express itself. Profound love doesn't lecture an unloved person with "Once you learn to love yourself, others will love you." No, profound love says, "I see you. I see that you don't yet know that you are dearly loved. I will love you and keep loving you until you are so clothed in love that being loved and loveable becomes your deepest truth."

Further, the Sacred Black Feminine's love is ever willing to go the distance to find us. She doesn't make us meet her halfway, in the middle of the ocean. She doesn't require us to be out consciously looking for her before she reveals herself to us. She doesn't require us to believe in her or trust her before she reveals herself to us. She doesn't require us to fully decolonize ourselves and rid ourselves of our colonial identities before she reveals herself to us. She comes to us, where we are and as we are. In pursuit of profound love, she'll cross an entire ocean for us and lovingly shape-shift into a being that we can both recognize and receive.

Even more, the Sacred Black Feminine's profound love for us leads her to be intentional about communicating her love in a way that resonates with us and is readily received by us.

Ever creative and shrewd, across history the Sacred Black Feminine has strategically appeared in ways that the culture can best receive her loving and liberating medicine. The story of Ọṣun and the people of Cuba is no different. As we take a deep dive into the story of Ọṣun in Cuba, we will discover just how cunning and strategic the Sacred Black Feminine is when it comes to demonstrating her love. We'll learn that the Sacred Black Feminine strategically demonstrated her love in five crucial ways:

One, Ọṣun strategically appeared as Black Madonna, a religious icon that was already revered in Cuba. In order to be recognized and received by Juan Moreno and the other enslaved people, who had been socialized to view the Divine through the lens of colonial Christianity, Ọṣun appeared to them as the Virgin Mary. But she didn't reveal herself as a pious, conservative, and boring white Virgin Mary. By bearing the title the Virgin of "Charity"—a Christian term for the highest form of love, the love between the Divine and humankind—Ọṣun as the Virgin Mary revealed her deeper self as Ọṣun the Yoruba orisha of love. In this way, the title the Virgin of Charity became an intimate and empowering secret between Ọṣun and her enslaved people, a reminder that beneath the Catholic, "respectable" veneer of the Virgin Mary lay the wild, daring, ocean-crossing, and passionate love of their beloved Ọṣun. She arrived as the Ọṣun-infused Black Madonna of Love, an updated, liberated version of the Virgin Mary—one that could accommodate and even celebrate the complex racial and religious identities of her diasporic people. Even today, Ọṣun's dual identity as the Yoruba orisha of love *and* the Virgin of Charity is evident in many handmade statues and folk paintings throughout the Cuban diaspora. Though the institutional church calls her the Virgin of Charity, and often depicts her as a prim and mild white Virgin Mary, on people's home altars she stands tall with bare breasts exposed, voluptuous hips tilted, a decidedly erotic energy, and the caramel skin color of the multiracial people of Cuba. By appearing as the Virgin of Charity, an image that the people could readily relate to and embrace, the Sacred Black Feminine powerfully and lovingly enabled her estranged people to say hello to their own Mother Ọṣun.

Two, Ọṣun strategically appeared to a multiracial child who could bridge the gap between the older and younger generations. As a second-generation Afro-Cuban, Juan Moreno likely had at least one parent who was full Yoruban. As such, he deeply connected to the older African generation as well as the younger, multiracial second generation. In this way, Juan's story appealed to and was credible to both dark-skinned enslaved people like his West African birth parent and caramel-colored, multiracial enslaved people like himself.

Three, Ọṣun strategically appeared to a relatively empowered member of the enslaved people. Since Juan was owned by the king of Spain, his status as a "royal slave" made him a reliable witness in the eyes of the ruling elite and a prominent spokesperson for Ọṣun. At the same time, by appearing to enslaved boys, Ọṣun made it resoundingly clear that she came for and stood in solidarity with the enslaved people.

Four, Ọṣun strategically appeared to both multiracial and Indigenous children. Alongside Juan Moreno, Ọṣun also appeared to Juan and Rodrigo de Hoyos, two Indigenous brothers who were also enslaved.[7] In doing so, Ọṣun signaled that she crossed oceans for *all* the colonized peoples of Cuba—Black, Indigenous, and multiracial. Through Ọṣun, the orisha of love, the Sacred Black Feminine universally embraced all people, including the people who did not hail from the Yoruba people of West Africa.

Five, Ọṣun strategically appeared while the boys were out mining for salt—a revelatory metaphor for how the Divine offers sweetness, freshness, and love to us, especially when life feels salty and bitter. If you recall, on the morning the boys encountered Ọṣun, they were harvesting salt to deliver to the salt mines during yet another arduous day of child labor. Imagine living the salty, bitter, inhumane life of an enslaved child, going about your normal, salty routine, and miraculously encountering an icon from the old country that promises sweetness, love, pleasure, and life. Of all the times Ọṣun, the orisha of the sweetwater riverways of Africa, could have appeared, she chose to appear to enslaved boys when they engaged in the particularly bitter task of harvesting salt. In doing so, she strategically pronounced her mission of love, beauty, and abundance. In this way, Ọṣun's appearance promised that despite all that her people had endured, she would exchange their salt for sweetness, their death for life, their pain for pleasure, and their scarcity for abundance. After they had spent years believing that they were forsaken, Ọṣun's miraculous arrival meant a new day and a new hope.

BLACK MADONNA, QUEEN OF LOVE-IN-ACTION

But Black Madonna doesn't just love her people; she also empowers and liberates her people. As soon as she appeared to the caramel-colored Juan, Ọṣun got busy doing what she does best: showing her beautiful people that they matter and empowering them to seize their worth and live life to the fullest. Though the people recognized her as Ọṣun, in many ways she embraced her disguise and second identity as the Black Madonna of Charity because this allowed her to more fully integrate into Cuban society and more effectively protect her people. And her first order of business was showing everyone that the enslaved people of El Cobre were not forsaken but were in fact her cherished children. One powerful way she proclaimed her solidarity with and love for the enslaved people of El Cobre was by physically abiding with them. Typically, miraculous Virgin Mary statues are placed in sophisticated places like the cathedral in a major city. But not this Black Madonna! She came to *dwell* among her enslaved people, not just *appear* to them. In addition to sharing their skin color and appealing to their Yoruba spiritual origins, Black Madonna took up residence in the makeshift sanctuary that the enslaved people crafted for her in their shantytown on the edge of El Cobre. By moving into the enslaved people's neighborhood and taking up permanent residence there, Black Madonna reaffirmed her commitment to the most marginalized people in colonial society.

Her second order of business was establishing herself as a powerful spiritual force on the island. Anyone who's read E. B. White's classic children's book *Charlotte's Web* knows that the best way to amass power is to perform miracles. In *Charlotte's Web*, a lowly and insignificant pig named Wilbur is faced with an existential threat: He's on his way to the slaughterhouse. So what does Wilbur, the runt of the litter, do to save himself? He enlists the help of Charlotte, a clever spider who lives in his pigpen. Over the course of several days, Charlotte weaves intricate webs over Wilbur's pen, and each web includes affirming marketing messages like "Some Pig," "Terrific," and "Radiant." The news of the "miraculous" pig who presided under these magical webs spreads all over the countryside, and Wilbur becomes such a sensation that his life is saved. Within a matter of several miraculous months, Wilbur goes from insignificant to celebrated, from doomed to protected.

Like Wilbur and Charlotte, Black Madonna understood that in a slaughter-happy colonial society, making miracles was the most strategic pathway to life-saving power and acclaim. Within days of inhabiting her makeshift sanctuary, Black Madonna began performing a series of miracles while under the nightly care of the de Hoyos brothers. During the darkest hour, she would inexplicably disappear, only to reappear at daybreak draped in sopping wet clothes. As you may recall, this is the exact inverse of the miracle she performed when she first appeared to Juan and Rodrigo de Hoyos and rose from the sea with perfectly dry clothes. Much like the story in *Charlotte's Web*, these miracles were essentially a PR campaign. As Black Madonna repeated this miracle over and over, word spread all over the island that a new Virgin Mary was on the scene and this was not any old Virgin Mary. This Virgin Mary was "Some Mary," "Terrific," and "Radiant." Within a matter of a few miraculous months, Black Madonna went from being the lowly Virgin Mary of the enslaved people to a celebrated spiritual icon. In this way, Black Madonna began to draw the attention of the island's powerful elite—and in doing so, she drew attention to the lives and plight of her beloved enslaved people of El Cobre.

Her third order of business was establishing herself as a powerful political force. As Black Madonna's acclaim grew and more people began visiting her humble makeshift sanctuary on the margins of El Cobre, she began performing practical miracles such as healing the sick and supplying rain in the midst of drought. At first, only the enslaved people venerated her, but as her spiritual power expanded, the civic and religious leaders of El Cobre began to covet the attention and financial gifts that her presence attracted to the enslaved people's shantytown. So the powerful El Cobre men decided to relocate Black Madonna's sanctuary to the parish church in the center of town. But Black Madonna spent the next three nights protesting her move by sending off puzzling night lights that terrorized the town officials. Afraid to offend her, they decided to build her a proper hermitage in the enslaved people's neighborhood, and this move cemented her political status as the protector of the enslaved people and their divine representative.[8]

As she continued to rise in influence and adoration, the most powerful whites on the island wanted to bring her closer to them in Santiago. Their colonial imaginations were so impoverished that they could not imagine that the enslaved multiracial, Black, and Indigenous people in the small mining village of El Cobre could possibly properly steward such an important religious icon. Plus the Cuban elite understood that Black Madonna's physical proximity to the enslaved people threatened the existing power system. They were worried that if she remained with the enslaved people, they would become so empowered by her that they would revolt. So the Cuban elite decided to transfer Black Madonna to the more metropolitan and sophisticated city of Santiago about ten miles away. With all the pomp and circumstance of a triumphant military parade, they carried Black Madonna in a dramatic procession to Santiago. But they did not even make it to the halfway point before Black Madonna simply disappeared into thin air. *Poof*—she was gone! Later, she reappeared at her sanctuary among the enslaved people of El Cobre. She insisted on remaining in El Cobre, among the enslaved people that she called her children, and there was nothing the so-called elite could do about it.[9] Over the years, whenever local officials forgot who they were dealing with and threatened to take Black Madonna away or prevent the people from praying to her, they would invariably be struck down, a reminder not to mess with the Virgin or her precious people.[10]

All of Black Madonna's political moves—appearing to and standing in solidarity with the enslaved people, amassing spiritual and political power in the eyes of both the enslaved people and the Cuban elite, and defiantly resisting the demands of the Cuban elite—were strategic steps toward empowering her people and helping them step into their identities as sacred. Not surprisingly, her well-laid plan worked. Over time, as Black Madonna's power grew, the enslaved people began to embody it and negotiate a better life for themselves. For example, the enslaved people of El Cobre leveraged her power to petition the king for more rights for themselves—such as the right for married couples and families to remain intact and not be separated and sold to other plantations, as well as the right to an accessible pathway to purchase their freedom. Through these rights, many of the enslaved people of El Cobre managed to keep their families intact and even gain their freedom. Later, when the king sold all the remaining enslaved people who worked in his plantation mines, the local governors sometimes did not comply with the king's pre-existing orders that the families remain intact. When this happened, the enslaved people would invoke Black Madonna's name in their petition to the local governor. The mere mention of her name would send shudders down the governor's spine and force the governor into compliance.

Black Madonna's relentless and loving pursuit of her people exemplifies the Spirit of God in the sacred book of Isaiah, who assured the abandoned ancient Hebrew people, "No longer will they call you Deserted . . . for you shall be called Sought After." Black Madonna's solidarity with the most marginalized Cuban people has had a lasting and liberating effect. By both crossing an ocean and changing her appearance to match the multiracial generations of Cubans, Black Madonna embodied a love so expansive, regenerative, and adaptable that it can reach any land and any people. Because the people knew that she had crossed an ocean for them, they knew without a shadow of a doubt that the orisha of love truly loved them. They knew that her love, power, and protection knew no bounds and that they could rely on it. To this day, the Black Madonna of Charity is known as a revolutionary mama, the one who declares that all people should be free and empowers the people to co-create a free world.

By transforming her dark, shimmering skin into a caramel color, Black Madonna redefined the concept of beauty to extend to all people who belong to her—whether they are dark-skinned people who look like Ọṣun, the orisha of love, or light-skinned people who look like the Black Madonna of Love. To Black Madonna, beauty is defined by belongingness rather than physical appearance. Since Black Madonna's Blackness contains all our skin colors—all belong to her, all can encounter their beauty in her, and all are worthy of dignity and freedom.

A LIMITLESS LOVE

She crosses oceans for you too, beloved.

But as she demonstrated with the Afro-Cuban people, she doesn't just cross oceans to love us; she crosses oceans to empower us. She's the Black Madonna of Love *and* Love-in-Action. Much like colonial Cuban society, our white patriarchal world loves to divide us into hierarchies and offer freedom and dignity to some people while violently denying it to others. Whether the hierarchies are interracial (e.g., white people are more valued and protected than Black people) or intraracial (e.g., light-skinned Black people are more valued and protected that dark-skinned Black people), or across gender, sexuality, ability, religion, class and other identity markers—white patriarchy knows how to make just about anyone feel excluded, unloved, unprotected, and unwanted. Further, white patriarchy loves to prey on the very insecurities that we inherited from its punitive hierarchy. White patriarchy tries to erase our connection to the Sacred Black Feminine by taunting us with unsettling thoughts such as:

Your imperfections are a burden and make you unlovable.

Your tantrums and dysregulated moments are unacceptable.

You don't meet society's impossible beauty and performance standards; therefore you are unworthy of belonging and protection.

Your story is unredeemable.

You are deserted.

Thank Goddess for the Sacred Black Feminine who relentlessly pursues us as the Black Madonna of Love and transforms our insecurities into belongingness. She's a shape-shifter when she needs to be because her infinite Blackness contains all colors and body types. Heck, her infinite Blackness contains all forms of molecules and can transform from sweet river water to rainwater that joins the salty sea. The most ancient and fervent of mothers, she'll shape-shift into any body and cross any ocean to assure us that, though white patriarchy may have called us *deserted*, we are in fact *sought after*. As the Black Madonna of Love, her primary vocation is to graciously pursue us, eagerly reminding us that no matter what our identity markers are or what society has tried to tell us, our deepest truths are that we belong to her, and that her beauty and our beauty are one and the same. We are beautiful because she is beautiful. We belong because we belong to her. We are wanted because she wants us and has pursued us since the beginning of time.

Imagine a world in which each and every human knows with every fiber of their embodied soul that they are beautifully divine and that they irrevocably belong to the Black Madonna of Love. Insecurity and the need for hierarchy and domination would fall away, and people would be motivated to generously share her expansive and inclusive love with all others. As people who are transformed by our belongingness to her, we would not tolerate systems of oppression such as transphobia, white supremacy, and ableism. Greed and resource scarcity would fall away because, as people who belong to the Black Madonna of Love, we wouldn't constantly fear for our survival. Rather than hoarding resources and colonizing lands, we would keep what we genuinely need for today and share the rest with our global neighbors. The circular gift-based economies of the ancient matriarchal societies would bloom again.

Imagine if *you* knew with every fiber of your embodied soul that you are beautifully divine and irrevocably belong to the Black Madonna of Love.

Would you look in your own story for how Black Madonna has crossed oceans for you? How would you hold your imperfections? How would you navigate uncertain times? How would you negotiate your freedom? Would you place your dysregulated self on the altar to a wild, passing God? Would you call yourself sought after? Would you fully answer your Mother's call?

MAPPING BLACK MADONNA'S
LOVING PURSUIT OF US

2020 was a hellish year, one that most of us would never choose to relive. And yet, it's the year that also taught me one of Black Madonna's most powerful truths: that the hope, peace, and trust I long for already exist within me, in my embodied memory. We often talk about how the body holds trauma. Yes, it does. But the body also holds hope, peace, and trust—if we're willing to seek it out. The culmination of my years of trauma therapy and intensive spiritual practice made it resoundingly clear that much of my life had been shaded by grief and pain, both personal and systemic. And though my grief- and pain-filled memories were easily accessible to me, I instinctively knew that grief and pain weren't my entire story. I wanted to spelunk my lifetime of memories and excavate the beauty, redemption, and hope that lay buried beneath my most accessible memories. I wanted to bring memories of beauty, redemption, and hope to the conscious surface and restore my inner well of hope, trust, and peace.

Toward the end of 2019, my spiritual director, Lourdes, and I began dreaming up a ritual to help me connect with the well of hope, trust, and peace in my embodied memory. I would turn 40 years old in 2020, and though I had only been a Black Madonna devotee for about five years, I believed that she had always been there for me—even before I knew to look for her, much less call out to her. In other words, just as Ọṣun donned a disguise, traveled across the ocean, and revealed herself as the Black Madonna of Love who would never abandon her people, I wanted to look for Black Madonna's presence in my life, paying special attention to the unlikely places where she had been in disguise.

I wanted to discover Black Madonna as a Holy Tracker who has been tracking me with the fierce intensity of a mother bear tracking her young.

As we know from the story of Ọṣun, Black Madonna is both a tracker *and* a shape-shifter; she can be found in nature, individuals, conversations, aha-moments, art, lessons learned the hard way, disappointment, bird-song, confusion, breakthroughs, grief, celebrations, and so much more. I decided to commemorate my 40 years on earth by scanning my memories across my lifespan and looking for the ways that Black Madonna actively cared for, parented, guided, protected, inspired, challenged, resourced, and accompanied me through it all—both the highs and the lows.

So on January 1, 2020, I began a daily, year-long practice in which I spent 15 minutes identifying and writing about an instance in which Black Madonna showed up for me, even before I had ever heard of her. I wrote each instance and reflection on a colorful card and affixed it to the wall around my fireplace, creating a mosaic mural. Since I did this practice every day during a leap year, I eventually collected 366 "Black Madonna memories." A diverse and even wacky collection, the memories included:

- Items—like a super-warm blanket an acquaintance gave me when he heard through the grapevine that my heater had died in the middle of a Minnesota winter and I had no money to fix it

- Expertise and help—like another acquaintance, an electrician who also heard about my broken heater and came over to fix it for free

- People—like the dean *from another school* who went out of his way to protect me and appeal to my dean on my behalf even though I was not on his faculty and certainly not his responsibility

- Consumables—like the bougie Mariage Frères tea that I discovered in France that was a literal gateway into pleasure and ease for me

- Wisdom and insight—like when I embraced what I call the Holy No, the sacred act of setting boundaries, relinquishing people-pleasing, and preserving space and energy for the things I actually feel called (not compelled) to do

- Clothing—like the pink-and-black striped set I wore almost every day when I was seven years old because I felt beautiful and unstoppable when I wore it

- Books—like Chanequa Walker-Barnes's *Too Heavy a Yoke: Black Women and the Burden of Strength* that had me crying by the end of the first paragraph and was a major catalyst on my liberation journey

- Music—like the Roberta Flack song "I Told Jesus" that my spiritual director introduced me to

- Bona fide miracles—like ongoing freedom from compulsive food behaviors; the breakthrough realization that the Divine is just as present in darkness, confusion, and pain; full scholarships and debt-free degrees; affordable housing in violently unaffordable markets; and insurance windfalls that came through in the nick of time, to name a few

- Many, many more—357 more to be exact.

By the time the COVID-19 pandemic reached the U.S. and the lock-downs began in March 2020, I was already several weeks into my daily Black Madonna practice. In other words, I was already deeply rooted in the myriad ways that Black Madonna had pursued me and revealed herself across my lifespan. As the horrors of 2020 unfolded—systemic ones like COVID and the murders of Breonna Taylor, George Floyd, Riah Milton, and Dominique "Rem'mie" Fells, as well as personal ones like divorce, separation from my biological family, and the isolation of lockdown—I found my Black Madonna practice to be a soothing and empowering counterpoint.

Each day as I encountered unprecedented hardships and pain, I also encountered evidence of her ever-present love in my life. As I reflected on all that she had done, even without my conscious awareness, I began to trust her with my current pain as well as the systemic pain of which I was unaware. Each day, as I wrote about yet another example in which she "crossed oceans for me" and manifested her power, creativity, and mercy in my life, I began to map Black Madonna's loving presence in my life. As the map filled in, I discovered that, like Ọṣun, she had never abandoned me and would cross any ocean for me. As the map developed, I became more convinced that I could trust her to continue crossing oceans for me.

Now it's your turn to map Black Madonna's loving pursuit in your own life.

As you reminisce about your life, it may be helpful to focus your scan in the following ways:

- Set a goal that feels accessible and life-giving for you. While I'm super intense and did this practice every day for a year, you may find a week or a fortnight to be sufficient. It's important to remember that though white patriarchy teaches us that "bigger is better" and "more is more," in Black Madonnaland, each and every action is treasured, nurtured, and multiplied by her infinite fertility.

- Depending on your age as well as your life story, you may find it helpful to focus your scan on a set number of years. For example, if your childhood was especially stormy, you may want to focus there. If you're in the throes of midlife and you're searching for Black Madonna in the here and now, you may want to focus your scan on the last five years.

- Consider focusing your scan on the good things that Ọṣun is traditionally known for: water, love, beauty, purity, divination, sexuality, destiny, and fertility.[11] If you follow this guideline, as you reminisce, you may become curious about how Black Madonna has revealed herself in these areas of your life.

Possible materials: multicolored paper, markers, tape, a pen

1. To ground yourself in the story of Ọṣun/Black Madonna, take a few moments to re-imagine her love for her people, her efforts to learn about her people's current needs, her appeal to her people, and the sacrifices she happily made in order to pursue her people.

2. Next, begin to map Black Madonna memories across your life. Can you identify an instance when a need was serendipitously met? What are the details of the need? How did you feel before the need was met? How did you feel afterward? Some areas to consider when spelunking for Black Madonna memories: items, expertise/help, people, consumables, wisdom/insight, clothing, books, music, bona fide miracles.

3. List and reflect on as many Black Madonna memories as feel good to you, attuning to your embodied wisdom to know when your list is complete for now.

4. What does it feel like to collect, name, and reflect on these memories? Did this practice impact your perception of Black Madonna, your life, or her presence in your life? If so, how?

5. If it is accessible to you, feel free to create a mosaic monument to your sacred history by writing each Black Madonna memory down on a different piece of paper and affixing it to a wall in your home.

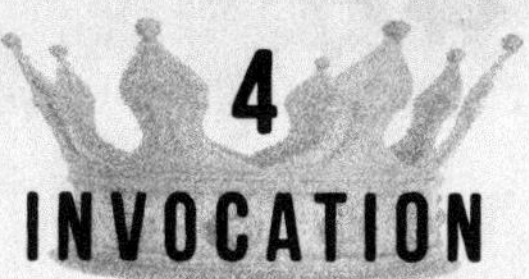

4
INVOCATION

Subterranean Lady who holds the world in balance
you beckon us, the under-mothered and overloaded
To swap our baggage for ease, oh supreme ease
In your unfathomably strong and bountiful arms.

Pregnant Virgin, keeper of the cosmic crypt
Neither void nor death can thwart your seed of life.
Impregnate us with your everlasting abundance
As our burdened and barren souls drink from your holy well.

Our Lady of the Labyrinth, you deftly deliver us
Just in the nick of time. When life's linear
booby-trapped maze is set to discourage and detonate,
You whisk us away to your circle, where love is ever in bloom.

Miracle-Working OB-GYN, our Resurrection Doula—
when toxic lies inseminate our body and soul,
you pull death from our womb and deliver nothing
But life, more life, indomitable life!

Spiral Seer, your cosmic hands are the gateway to life.
You guide each stride, assuring your dear ones
that every direction—north, south, east, or west—
Is anointed, tended, and lavished by you.

Chapter 4

SHE MOTHERS US INTO ABUNDANCE

Encountering Ease Along Black Madonna's Life-Giving Labyrinth

Black women know a thing or two about heavy burdens.

The burdens that Black women carry are so profound, so layered, so transgenerational, and so unfathomable that we often need others to help us recognize them and truly feel the magnitude of their weight. I can still remember the first time I listened to jessica Care moore's searing choreopoem "We Want Our Bodies Back." My body shook as she named the nervous breakdowns that ravage our minds and fibroids that terrorize our uteruses—a visceral reminder that though "Black don't crack," we definitely crack on the inside. As Care moore put words to the heavy tradition of Black women buying black funeral dresses, my imagination immediately carried me to the many tragic and untimely funerals I've attended. When she named the reality that lynchings still happen today, I shuddered at the memory of Jamar Clark, a young Black man who was murdered by police in 2015, just three blocks from my Minneapolis condo. By painfully and meticulously listing burden after burden, Care moore paints a picture of a society that "has sucked the life out of countless, miscounted, uncounted brown poor women."[1]

Black women carry the burden of our ancestors in our bodies, the burden of the plantation ripping Black mothers from their children in our broken relationships, the burden of police brutality and mass incarceration in our grief, the burden of the racial-gender wage gap in our bank accounts, the burden of white jesus in our toxic commitment to suffering, and the burden of contemporary misogynoir in our compulsions, addictions, and exasperated nervous systems.

Despite our immense burdens, most Black women are also severely *under-mothered*. In other words, when our burdens exceed our capacity and we are in need of guidance, assurance, and resources, many Black women are left to fend for ourselves. No one is there to support us when we need it. Since the median wealth in Black households is less than one-sixth the median wealth in white households,[2] and Black family dynamics have been strategically sabotaged since the period of enslavement, Black women are rarely able to turn to family members to ease their financial or emotional burdens. And in a society that insists on perceiving Black women as superhuman and shames us if we show even a sliver of vulnerability, we certainly cannot expect any life-giving safety nets from social and governmental institutions.

Further, many Black women are discovering that we cannot look to the church to ease our burdens either. Though Black Americans, and Black women in particular, are deeply religious and have lingered in institutional church spaces, we are beginning to leave. Recent research shows that Black women, especially Black women who have left historically Black Christian denominations, are much more likely to hold "New Age" beliefs than white women. The Black church exodus is so vast that religious studies professor Tamura Lomax's research is focused on Black women leaving Black and non-Black church spaces due to rampant patriarchy and white supremacy. Even in our spiritual spaces, Black women are tragically under-mothered. Nevertheless, we are asked to mother *everyone else*. Despite the fact that no one is holding us, we are required to single-handedly hold our communities together. The burdens Black women carry as *community mothers* are typically unseen, unacknowledged, unappreciated, and ungrieved. So naturally I screamed when I first read Donna Kate Rushin's "The Bridge Poem" in which she describes the overwhelming burdens that Black women carry as translators, mediators, and peacekeepers who stand at the intersection of multiple racial, gender, religious, and economic realities.

Speaking from personal experience, Rushin offers a dizzying list of people who, trapped in their homogenous reality, rely on her to navigate a diverse world. Her parents use her as the go-between messenger in their marital conflicts. Her father and brother can only relate to her sister if Rushin intervenes. The white feminists don't know how to collaborate with the Black church folks unless Rushin is there to mediate. The Black church folks can't work with the Black separatists unless Rushin is involved and playing the role of peacekeeper. The ex-hippies rely on Rushin to help them understand the Black church folks *and* the Black separatists. The artists don't know how to foster a meaningful conversation with her friend's parents unless Rushin brokers it. And in the midst of it all, Rushin has to also explain herself to all these groups of people. Exasperated, she concludes:

I do more translating
Than the Gawdamn U.N.[3]

Parentified since birth, Black women labor under the weight of our unbearable pain, a dearth of mothering across all aspects of our lives, and immense community needs. Though we may have been praised for our strength and independence in our youth, as we grow into adulthood, our faithful, overburdened, seemingly superhuman bodies eventually reveal themselves as human and begin to crumble. Even if our physical appearance somehow, mysteriously conforms to the dehumanizing stereotype that "Black don't crack," we find ourselves cracking on the inside. Eventually, we are compelled to cry out:

Hellllooooo.

Is anybody out there?

Is anybody holding me and guiding me as I walk this booby-trapped maze of life?

Is anybody mothering me as I mother everyone else?

From the depths of her ancient crypt, Our Lady of the Underworld, the Black Madonna of Chartres, France, responds with a resounding and absolute *Yes, yes, yes, my child! I have been here holding, guiding, and mothering you since the beginning of time. Step onto my life-giving labyrinth, release your burdens, and let me mother you into abundance.*

OUR LADY OF THE UNDERWORLD HOLDS IT ALL SO WE DON'T HAVE TO

At first glance, Our Lady of the Underworld doesn't seem like a Black Madonna who offers much abundance. If you visit her lightless and cold crypt, the first thing you will notice is how dark, dank, and seemingly inhospitable it is. It feels like a bomb shelter; the cavernous walls that surround Our Lady of the Underworld are made of rough-hewn rock. And the pungent aroma that fills the space is reminiscent of a moldy basement on a humid summer day. Yet it is bizarrely frigid down there. No matter the season, I never visit the crypt without a jacket because the damp, cool air makes my teeth chatter. Consistent with the underwhelming environs, her wooden statue is simple, small, and set in a dimly lit corner of the large crypt. Unlike many other Black Madonnas, she isn't intricately carved, lavishly enrobed, or even painted. Rather, her simple pearwood body sits on an unremarkable throne with her child on her lap.

But despite appearances, this ancient Black Madonna has been offering her profound life force to humans for millennia. Long before the birth of Christ, the ancient Druids worshipped a dark goddess who lived next to a well in a grotto just beneath the surface of Chartres Cathedral. But this was no ordinary goddess, well, or grotto—for they were on a ley line, a prehistoric track connecting ancient landmarks and spiritually significant sites. According to spiritualists, ley lines carry the flow of our own life-current as well as the energy of the cosmos, and sites that exist on ley lines are ripe with supernatural power. Though ley lines are invisible and cannot be confirmed by scientific methods, they have been detected by dowsers and others who are sensitive to energetic forces. Even the most cynical among us will probably find it fascinating that the goddess, well, and grotto are said to exist on a ley line called "the Rose Line" that links the sacred sites of Glastonbury, Stonehenge, and the pyramids of Egypt. As Chartres sits between these three sites, it is said that all the powerful spiritual energies of Glastonbury, Stonehenge, and the pyramids converge at the Chartres goddess, grotto, and well. Though the ancient Druids probably lacked intellectual knowledge of ley lines and merging spiritual forces, they must have implicitly understood that this grotto, well, and goddess were miraculously generative and extremely powerful—for they called the goddess "Virgini Pariturae," which means "the Virgin with child." Due to the physical healing and spiritual empowerment that people reliably experienced at the altar of the Pregnant Virgin, the grotto eventually became the Druids' most important sanctuary in all of Gaul (pre-Roman France).

Long after Christianity colonized central France and the Chartres Cathedral was built atop this ancient goddess site, the people continued to worship their Pregnant Virgin in the grotto beneath the cathedral and receive physical and spiritual healing from her magical well. Over the centuries, as Catholicism attempted to distance itself from its pagan origins, the grotto was sanitized and turned into a crypt, the well was closed off, and the ancient dark goddess was recast as the Virgin Mary. Early Christians called her the Blessed Subterranean Lady, but later she was christened as Our Lady of Chartres and incorporated into the spiritual practices of the medieval Catholic Church as a Black Madonna.[4] Regardless of Black Madonna's name or religious affiliation, her sacred well remained powerful. Even when it was Christianized, it was still called the "well of the holy strong ones" because all who received its water were immediately empowered.[5] Despite the efforts of the Catholic Church to squelch the ancient Druidic spirituality, the people always remembered the deeper magic and continued passing through the airy, well-lit upper cathedral, past the white jesus on the main altar, and down into the dank crypt, where they knew they would encounter the ley line–infused, subterranean life force they needed.

Today Our Lady of the Underworld remains in the crypt of Chartres Cathedral, her body a clarion call to a more abundant life. Like many Black Madonnas, what she offers us can be found in the details of her story and her statue. For example, the child sitting on her lap isn't a stationary newborn or even an unsteady toddler. Rather, he looks like an active and ready-to-roam four-year-old and sits sprightly perched on the very edge of her lap. Her hands on his hips, she steadies and guides his movement—as if she knows that, despite his independence, he needs her.

Our Lady of the Underworld, like many Black Madonnas, has exceptionally large hands. Historian and theologian Annine van der

Meer invites us to take note of this unique quality. She writes, "In the Middle Ages they were able to master the technique of perfectly expressing the right proportions, so enlarging is not a question of technical inability, but is rather an indication of something else. It has to do with symbolic meaning . . . the larger the hands, the stronger the forces will be that are transferred via the hands."[6] Medieval Black Madonna devotees believed that Black Madonna's large hands transferred magnetic earth forces and could restore physical ailments and even resurrect stillborn babies. Though this profound belief is unique in the Christian world, it is not a new belief but a continuation of the world's earliest spiritualities. Our ancient African ancestors believed that the Sacred Black Feminine's hands were the gateway to life.[7]

Our Lady of the Underworld's loving grip on her child's hips doesn't just steady and guide him; it also bolsters his life force and brings restoration to his world. Holding nothing back, she offers all of the ancient energy that flows through her everlasting and boundless spring. Every good and restorative element that flows through her—love eternal, the deep wisdom of the ancients, groundbreaking physical remedies, immortal seeds of joy, a peace that passes all understanding, ecstatic wonder, the brilliance of the stars, indescribable pleasure, the unshakable stability of the earth's core, the explosive force of the volcano, the calm courage of a mature lion, and the purity of an infant's giggle—is channeled through her large hands and into her child's being. And like her underground well, her life force is eternal. No matter what he faces as he outgrows her lap and saunters into adulthood, her cosmic hands hold it all so he doesn't have to. Forever steadying his hips, guiding his every step, she channels abundance from her well of holy strong ones into every aspect of his life.

Our Lady of the Underworld offers every good and restorative element to us too. For she doesn't just hold her child in her miraculously life-giving hands; she holds us too. You see, directly above the crypt, in the main sanctuary of the breathtakingly beautiful cathedral, lies the Chartres labyrinth. The most famous labyrinth in the world, millions of pilgrims walk its sacred path each year, offering their deepest questions, angst, challenges, and malaise to the Divine. The labyrinth is powerful and renowned because Our Lady of the Underworld upholds the labyrinth with her cosmic hands. As if her hands are on our hips too, her life force from the crypt below steadies our journey on life's labyrinth and offers us every good and restorative element. She is down in the dank crypt holding it down so we can walk the light-filled, spacious, and climate-controlled labyrinth above her. We don't have to labor in the crypt with her. She wants us to enjoy life, and she's doing the work of holding it all together so that we don't have to.

MOTHERED BY BLACK MADONNA'S LABYRINTH

Our Lady of the Underground's labyrinth is symbolically rich. It was created in the 12th century, when most pilgrims were illiterate, and many of the labyrinth's spiritual truths were communicated with symbols. For example, the four quadrants of the labyrinth represent the seasons, assuring pilgrims that they are divinely held and guided through highs and lows, life and death, and the fruitful and fallow seasons of life. Additionally, the cardinal points of north, south, east, and west promise pilgrims that everything is held by her cosmic hands and nothing escapes her expansive attention. The 113 dots around the edge of the labyrinth, which are called "lunations," correspond to the 114 of days in a lunar cycle. (There are 113 rather than 114 because one is intentionally excluded at the labyrinth's entrance.[8]) The lunations remind pilgrims that each and every day matters to Our Lady of the Underworld, that she is just as invested in channeling life into the minutiae of our lives as she is invested in channeling life into the major events. She offers her life force every day, not just on the days that seem important or urgent to us.

The fact that Our Lady of the Underworld guides our walk along life's labyrinth has deep and healing significance, especially for those of us who are tragically under-mothered. For one, Our Lady of the Underworld declares that life is a labyrinth, not a booby-trapped maze. Prolific labyrinth guide Regina Renee Nyégbeh makes an important distinction between labyrinths and mazes.[9] Unlike mazes, which are designed to befuddle, block, and frustrate, labyrinths are designed to guide and support. Because labyrinths are hedgeless, we enter them with a clear view of the journey. Additionally, mazes have dead ends that are designed to stymie your movement and prevent you from finding your way out. These dead ends affirm the white patriarchal belief that if we want to experience success and goodness, we must not ever make a wrong turn or get lost. But labyrinths, which only have one way in and one way out, liberate us from the fear that a wrong turn will set us back. In the labyrinth we can breathe a sigh of relief that there is no way to get lost. Despite all the twists and turns, as long as we follow the path, we will eventually arrive at the center of the labyrinth as well as find our way out. In a punitive society and in legalistic spiritual communities that often hold Black women to unrealistic standards of perfection, the labyrinth declares that any step in any direction is a holy step that is wholly held by Black Madonna.

Citing wisdom from a sermon by her beloved late father, Nyégbeh reminds us that Black Madonna's unflinching grip on our life labyrinth assures us that we are never lost; we simply need to receive the guidance and direction that is always available to us.[10] The labyrinth invites us to experience the divine mothering that the Hebrew psalmist melodically chanted about thousands of years ago: "Your hand sustains me; your loving care empowers me. You support my every movement, and my body does not give way."[11] Even more, Our Lady of the Underworld's labyrinth releases us from the rat race of linearity, which is a figment of the white patriarchal imagination. Her labyrinth path, which sometimes turns toward the center and sometimes turns away from it, assures us that we have not lost ground if we find ourselves taking two steps forward and one step back. When we surrender to her labyrinth path, each step, no matter the direction, leads toward the center, where we encounter union with her and all those around us. Similarly, her labyrinth, which continuously spirals throughout the course of our lives, assures us that we have not failed if we need to learn a lesson a second, third, or even ninth time. Rather than torturing ourselves with perfectionism and unrealistic performance goals, we can follow Jungian analyst and Black Madonna teacher Marion Woodman's invitation to relax and take pleasure in the journey of the spiral, trusting that if we are meant to learn something, we will—either on this trip around the labyrinth or a later one. We can relax and simply enjoy communion with Black Madonna on the spiral.

The labyrinth held by Black Madonna assures us that we are never alone and never under-mothered. Speaking of Black Madonna's guiding power, Ean Begg writes, "The light of nature tells us that life is a pilgrimage, a journey to the stars along the Milky Way, her hero-path, a voyage across the great water in which she is the ship, rudder, and guiding star. As the spirit of light in darkness she comes to break the chains of those who live in the prison of unconsciousness and restore them to their true home."[12] Our Lady of the Underworld's life-giving hands are always steadying us. Our Lady of the Underworld's life-giving hands are always awakening and grounding us. Our Lady of the Underworld's life-giving hands are always guiding us home to her. Our Lady of the Underworld's life-giving hands are always channeling every good and restorative element to us every single day. Our Lady of the Underworld's life-giving hands are always offering the sacred well water that transforms us into holy strong ones. Our Lady of the Underworld's life-giving hands are always holding it all so we don't have to. Always.

BLACK MADONNA'S ABUNDANCE

Within Our Lady of the Underworld's labyrinth, we also receive insight about what type of abundance Black Madonna offers. These days the word *abundance* gets tossed around a lot, and it's easy to believe that abundance is primarily or even exclusively a physical entity. If you listen to best-selling self-help authors or watch marketing webinars, you may equate abundance with a six- or seven-figure income, the complete lack of pain or hardship, or impeccable physical and mental ability—the factors that falsely promise greater acceptance by the white patriarchal powers that govern our society. Though Black Madonna is renowned for ushering physical abundance into people's lives, she isn't interested in helping us become more sanitized and acceptable to the colonial world. She knows that prominence and societal acceptance do not equal significance and that no amount of physical wealth will heal the deep trauma that comes from being overburdened and under-mothered. To put it in historical African American terms, Black Madonna isn't interested in helping us become the most powerful negroes *on* the plantation; she's devoted to helping us get *off* the plantation. So simply patching us up, helping us achieve societal acceptability, and depositing funds into our bank account isn't her end goal. Rather, her end goal is our freedom, and that goes way beyond the physical reality.

To Black Madonna, abundance isn't a dollar amount, an academic pedigree, a number of social media followers, a professional title, a well-stocked nuclear fortress, or social acceptability. Rather, abundance is *enoughness*—the deeply satisfying and grounding assurance that we have what we need to embody peace, generosity, and courage for today. When we are rooted in Black Madonna's abundance, we no longer regret the past, nor do we worry about the future. We are free to be fully present to today, to enjoy the pleasure of the spiral with her, to vulnerably receive the wisdom of her cosmic breast milk for today's challenges and opportunities, and to move through our day with courage, generosity, and hope. Black Madonna's abundance invites us to daily receive her mothering, release our burdens to her, and receive joy and ease—no matter what is going on around us. Black Madonna is the mother we have longed for, and her labyrinth is the nurturing lap that assures us that we are enough and have enough.

Black Madonna's abundance is subversive and will perhaps befuddle at first. She may not offer us what we *think* we need, but she will offer us what we *actually* need for today—whether that is courage to trust another day, a community with whom to weather the storm, emotional stability, financial resources, miraculous physical healing, a quiet sense of relief, shelter, the gift of peace, contagious joy, food that nourishes the body and soul, a creative solution to a persistent problem, a calming assurance, a new perspective, unflappable significance in the face of failure, self-love after rejection, a palpable feeling of divine accompaniment, strategic wisdom to take the next holy step, resurrected hope, and/or practical protection. Her abundance comes from the profound wisdom of her ancient well, the cosmic strength of hands that have held life's labyrinth since the beginning of time, and her infinite Blackness that contains all things, has seen all things, and is overburdened by absolutely nothing.

What form abundance takes will vary from person to person, depending on their personality, culture, and history. Thankfully,

Black Madonna has been lovingly mothering us our entire lives and understands our traumas, idiosyncrasies, and unique needs. As Begg writes: "Sometimes She comes to us in dreams and visions, in sickness cured, in rescue from catastrophe and in chance encounters with the numinous."[13] When we are overburdened, the labyrinth invites us to look beyond what we have been conditioned to believe about ourselves and our world, and seek Black Madonna's abundance. It may not look like a miracle. It may not look like a pot of gold at the end of a rainbow. It may not even offer us the tidy answers that we are conditioned to crave. But we will encounter her abundance if we seek it. And it will clothe us in surprising and unconventional ways that allow us to keep moving toward love, even with all that is going on around us. With each step on the labyrinth path, Black Madonna offers us a bespoke "abundance care package." She knows how to give us what we need so that we feel truly held and guided by her, can relax and enjoy the spiral of life's labyrinth, and can pass her abundance onto others.

SHE MOTHERS US WHEN LIFE FEELS LIKE A BOOBY-TRAPPED MAZE

Historian Marcus Bull, in his book *The Miracles of Our Lady of Rocamadou,* shares an unforgettable story about Black Madonna's abundant intervention in an excruciatingly painful situation.[14] During the 1200s, in the South of France, a young pregnant woman began to experience contractions as her due date approached. It seemed like a normal labor and delivery process at first. Her contractions became more frequent and intense as she labored in pain for hours and hours and then days and days. Of course, some birthing parents labor for longer than a day and some may do so for several days, but usually the baby eventually arrives—not so with this woman. She experienced harrowing birthing contractions every day after day after day until the days turned into weeks and the weeks turned into months and the months turned into years.

Yes, years. The woman was in labor every single hour of every single day for two-and-a-half years.

The situation was so dire that the woman began to lose her life force and will to live. In fact, the woman's parents, who witnessed their daughter's extreme pain, were "tormented by great sorrow and constantly grieved for their daughter just as if she were already dead." Naturally, the woman and her caring community were perplexed by the unprecedented and horrific illness. As news spread of this "new and unbearable sickness," the women's good-hearted neighbors responded with energetic compassion. Deeply devoted to Christianity, they gathered around her, mobilized the medieval equivalent of a meal train, and prayed with her. And as humans are wont to do when life feels like a booby-trapped maze, they tried to make sense of the women's senseless suffering.

If only this desperate community knew that Black Madonna was holding their life labyrinth and wanted to abide with them and guide them as they navigated an excruciating and uncertain situation. If only these earnest people knew of Black Madonna's life-giving well and her extraordinary ability to restore even the most unprecedented and horrifying experiences. If only this community knew that Black Madonna could breathe her abundant life into their hopeless situation. If only this community knew that Black Madonna's stabilizing roots were deeper than their destabilizing uncertainty and that they simply needed to dig deeper to encounter them. If only. But unfortunately these community members lived in the South of France, far away from any major Black Madonna sanctuaries, and had barely heard of her. So they continued scratching their heads in angst and searching for answers to their collective pain because that's what we humans do when we feel lost in life's labyrinth.

Social psychology research teaches us that the need to know is one of the most powerful needs that humans possess and is on par with basic physical needs, such as the need for air and the need for water. Humans are notoriously uncomfortable with uncertainty, especially when we are in the midst of transition, facing unknown situations, or experiencing distress. Due to our collective aversion to uncertainty, we feel extreme unease in the face of ambiguity. In fact, our discomfort is so great that we are motivated to reduce it by seeking out and embracing answers. We usually begin by looking to science for certainty because it often provides tidy answers that soothe our restless minds and banish our discomfort. But when our powerful need to know is not met by scientific facts, we look to spirituality to help steady us. When we are desperate, trapped in pain and can't explain it away, and do not possess the power to deliver ourselves, questions like *Where is the Divine when we are lost and in pain?* and *Can we count on divine wisdom to guide us to life?* often burst to the surface like volcanic eruptions.

Unfortunately, these questions don't typically usher us into the arms of a loving, abundant divine being who steadies our inner and outer worlds—and reminds us that life is a labyrinth, not a booby-trapped maze. In the midst of our distress, the white patriarchal god exploits our need for certainty and tries to convince us to resolve our discomfort by falling into shame, legalism, fundamentalism, control, and resignation. As chronically under-mothered people who haven't yet discovered that we are not alone and that we are constantly guided and resourced, we panic and revert to the old, terrorizing beliefs that white patriarchy has ingrained in us.

"See, you deserve this pain," the white patriarchal god whispers. "You must have made a wrong turn in the maze at some point and now you are lost and alone. You may never find your way out, so you might as well accept that your life is doomed to all pain and zero joy or ease."

So it's only natural that the woman's two-and-a-half-year labor triggered a powerful need within the entire community to know why this was happening and where God was in the midst of it all. But like most patriarchal religious communities that have long silenced the divine feminine, their questions didn't open them to a spacious and abundant divine being who could lovingly guide them through the twists and turns of life's labyrinth. Their questions didn't initially guide them into the loving arms of Black Madonna. No, their questions led them to drum up, regurgitate, and circulate harmful and misogynistic ideas about the Divine, women, and suffering. For example, in their attempt to make sense of the situation, the villagers became convinced that the Divine was actually the cause of the woman's pain, declaring, "The Lord's dreadful scourge terrifies everyone, especially when it bears down more severely than usual…" According to these community members, sometimes "God" is just extra scary and especially horrible and that's why the woman was suffering. But they didn't stop there; they also offered a spiritual justification for the woman's suffering, saying, "In this poor wretch was fulfilled the condemnation passed on the first woman: in pain shall you bring forth." According to these community members, this woman's extraordinary and dehumanizing anguish was simply her spiritual duty as a woman because this is how women must pay for Eve's "original sin" in the ancient Garden of Eden.

As they say, with friends like these, who needs enemies? Though this woman was surrounded by a well-meaning family and community, she remained severely under-mothered.

Imagine being a woman in labor for years—exhausted, barely able to breathe, almost entirely stripped of your life force—and being told that your pain is due to a terrifying god who inexplicably decided to be even more terrifying to you, and also that this is happening to you because you're a woman and the terrifying god has cursed all women. As you can probably imagine, the patriarchal "explanations" of these well-meaning community members did not help lighten the woman's emotional load or help her connect with the Black Madonna of the Underworld, who offers abundant life. As the months in labor continued and she sank deeper and deeper into despair, the woman understandingly began to lose her will to live. "She waited for death, although death is a bitter thing; and she screamed out that people who died were the lucky ones. Hers was a living death: she reckoned that death would be sweeter than her illness because it would last but a moment."

When all hope seemed lost, the woman's parents experienced a tide-turning aha moment! You see, years earlier they had journeyed to a Black Madonna sanctuary about 160 miles away, a vast distance to traverse during medieval times. They were so moved by their visit with Black Madonna that they donated a significant sum of money to help support the daily operations of the sanctuary. But over time they seemed to have forgotten about her, for it wasn't until 30 months into their daughter's suffering that they looked beyond the patriarchal god of their community and sought the intervention of the gracious

Black Madonna they had visited years before. Who better to call on when life feels like a booby-trapped maze than Black Madonna, who offers abundance, guidance, relief, and ease in the midst of it all?

As soon as the woman's parents prayed to Black Madonna, she instantly appeared in the woman's home in the South of France, performed a groundbreaking C-section procedure, and relieved the woman of her two-and-a-half-year hell. According to the story, "The woman's navel miraculously opened up—something which was contrary to nature and beyond the experience of mortal men—and the baby boy, by now long dead and decaying, was taken out piece by piece." Black Madonna miraculously took the death that had been burdening the woman for months and restoratively replaced it with ease and even joyful gumption!

Over the following weeks, the woman fully recovered and was even well enough to embark on the long, 160-mile pilgrimage to give thanks to Black Madonna in person. But beyond a physical transformation, the woman, who had been conditioned to believe that her plight as a woman was to suffer in silence, also experienced a spiritual transformation. By the time she arrived at Black Madonna's sanctuary, she had become so brazen and empowered that as she extolled the miraculous workings of Black Madonna, she happily and scandalously pulled up her skirt to expose her healed navel to anyone who was willing to witness it. "Being quite without shame, she showed off her wound, which was still open, and eloquently spoke in praise of the supreme Virgin." She was no longer a disempowered woman who drank the Kool-Aid of the patriarchal religious leaders, internalized their teachings about a misogynistic god who intentionally tortures women, and resigned herself to a life of tortuous pain. Instead, she became a bold preacher in her own right, proclaiming her truth in service to the fiercely liberating Black Madonna, who relieved rather than caused her pain. She couldn't stop telling everyone about Black Madonna, who holds it all so that we don't have to.

When no one else could mother the woman, Black Madonna mothered her.

When no one else could relieve the woman's pain, Black Madonna relieved it.

When her community was convinced that life is a booby-trapped maze, Black Madonna showed her that every single moment is lovingly guided.

When her community wanted her to accept a life of continuous torment, Black Madonna ushered in liberating abundance.

When the community wanted her to stay small, Black Madonna empowered her to take up space and share the good news that our lives are divinely supported.

RELEASING OUR BURDENS AND RECEIVING EASE

When I first read this astonishing story, I gasped. For months the woman suffered because she didn't know that a divine being wanted to accompany her in her ordeal, much less deliver her from it. For months, the woman suffered because she had been convinced that she was not only abandoned by God but actually attacked by him. For months, the woman carried death within her body because she didn't know that Black Madonna's large hands are capable of resuscitating stillborn babies. For months, the woman remained small and parroted the voice of the patriarchal church because that's what women were supposed to do. This jaw-dropping story about Black Madonna drives home how much we suffer when we believe that life is a booby-trapped maze and there is no one to help us, guide us, or offer us abundance.

It's worth noting that this is a very disturbing story, especially for those who have experienced birthing trauma. It may be helpful to interpret the story as an allegory about how Black Madonna wants to bring us ease, joy, and empowerment in a world that often dooms us to endless suffering. Though this story is set in the 1200s, many of us still carry the medieval woman's same toxic theology of suffering today. Perhaps you're like me and can relate to the woman in this story. I too have spent months and even years in anguish because my spiritual community convinced me that I deserved pain, obligation, and a joyless existence. Like the woman in the story, we often bear the burden of suffering because we have been taught that suffering is a pathway to significance or because we are convinced that our burdens are truly ours to carry. Like the woman in the story, we were not aware that we could call on a divine being to hold us, guide us, and offer a well of abundance in the midst of overwhelming pain and uncertainty. We were not taught that Our Lady of the Underworld is holding it all so that we don't have to.

But Black Madonna offers another way. As Begg writes, "The Black Virgin reminds us that we have an alternative, and that not all roads lead to Rome."[15] This story is an invitation to scan the landscape of our lives, searching for the instances in which we are needlessly suffering because we are trapped in the conditioning of the under-mothered, convinced that we have to carry every burden that life sends our way and unaware of the cosmic abundance of Black Madonna.

It's also worth noting that, as this story reveals, Black Madonna's labyrinth doesn't promise us a painless life. (Though, as we'll come to see in Chapter 6, she does promise to transform our pain, if we allow her to.) But more often than not, like the woman who labored for two-and-a-half years, we often needlessly suffer in ways that can be released to Black Madonna. As Buddhist teachers like Rev. angel Kyodo williams enlighten us, though pain is unavoidable, suffering is absolutely avoidable. Pain is inevitable because it is part of the birth/death/rebirth cycle of our natural world. But suffering is caused by our reaction to the inevitability of pain.[16] We suffer when we try to avoid, minimize, or become attached to our pain. Rather than being present to our pain and offering it to Black Madonna's labyrinth, we try to manipulate it with numbing behaviors or by avoiding experiences and risks that may cause us pain.

For example, it's extremely painful to witness a beloved adult in our life who is making unhealthy choices that cause them harm. This is the unavoidable pain of being a human adult in community with other human adults who possess the free will to make their own choices. But we add the unnecessary burden of suffering to our inescapable pain when we try to avoid the pain by never entering into close relationships with people or by attempting to shame the person into making different choices. Sometimes, we become attached to the pain by obsessively thinking about the person and abandoning our own needs as we do everything we can to shield them from the consequences of their choices. By trying to manipulate our pain, we pile on burdens that we were never meant to carry.

Other examples of burdens we were never meant to carry are:

- Taking on too much responsibility and not asking for what we need because we want to avoid the pain of being let down by people

- Staying in an unhealthy job, relationship, or community and avoiding steps in a life-giving direction because we are afraid that the risk will result in pain

- Playing it safe and small because believing in ourselves and trying something new may result in painful failure

- Drowning in shame because we have become so attached to our shame that we fear that if we release it, we will experience a painful identity crisis

- Excessive worry about the future because we believe that life is a booby-trapped maze, and we believe that worry will help us outsmart and avoid the pain

- Compulsively prioritizing other people's needs over our own because we fear that if we don't meet their needs, no one will

- Compulsive behaviors that temporarily numb our pain but clog our spiritual pipes and prevent us from receiving healing water from Black Madonna's sacred well

- Harmful generational patterns that we cling to because they give us a false sense of identity and connection to our family of origin

- Fear and anxiety when we are unable to control ourselves and others because we believe that we must hold it all

Though I have identified some examples of burdens here, many of the burdens we carry go unseen, unacknowledged, and ungrieved and may feel invisible to us. Many of us have carried burdens and cumbersome behavioral patterns for so long that they feel like a part of who we are, like a limb that we cannot imagine living without. We are often so accustomed to carrying them that when we awaken to Black Madonna's labyrinth and desire to pass our burdens on to her, we may not intuitively know how to identify our burdens, much less how to deftly release them in the midst of a crisis.

If you don't know how to identify and release your burdens, don't fret! For within her very name, Black Madonna is showing us how to do this. In her writings on Black Madonna's expansive mothering power, Marion Woodman makes a profound connection between the English word *matter* and the Latin word *mater*, which means "mother." She writes, "The fear of annihilation, carried in the cells of the abandoned child in many of us, makes us cling to matter as if that were the *mater* we have lost or never had."[17] Drawing on the fact that mater is an ancient name for the Sacred Black Feminine and that Black Madonna bears the Christianized title of Mater Dei (Mother of God), Woodman is showing us that anytime we find ourselves preoccupied with matter, we are really longing for Black Madonna. In other words, when we are in dire straits and most in need of the stabilizing and nurturing guidance of Black Madonna's labyrinth, we become attached to or preoccupied with things (people, our own behavior or other people's behavior, relationships, money, failure, what people think about us, or our bodies, for example) in a futile attempt to avoid pain and meet our mothering need.

And this is how we know we are carrying burdens that we were never meant to carry. When we find ourselves obsessing over what they're doing, what they need, what we are afraid of, what we don't have, what we currently have but don't want to lose, our imperfections, the future, or anything else that repeatedly runs laps in our mind—we can stop and remind ourselves that we are actually desperately longing for Black Madonna. We can pivot away from continuing to obsess over matter and instead open to the Mother we long for. We can step away from ruminating our way through the booby-trapped maze and step onto Black Madonna's life-giving labyrinth, where we release our burdens and receive her ease and joy in exchange.

Beloved, Black Madonna wants to perform a groundbreaking C-section on you too.

When we are experiencing unavoidable pain, we do not have to pile on the burden of suffering by clinging to matter. Instead, we can notice our need for the Mother, remain present to the pain, and invite Black Madonna to hold it with us and for us. When we open our most painful experiences to Black Madonna, she deftly removes the additional burdens of suffering that are not ours to carry and offers us her labyrinth path, which is just waiting to blow our minds and open us to new ways of being divinely mothered. In exchange for the burden of suffering, we get to open to the mystery of Black Madonna holding us in a unique and unimaginable way.

Begg affirms, "Underneath all of our conditioning, hidden in the crypt of our being, near the waters of life, the Black Virgin is enthroned with her Child, the dark latency of our own essential nature."[18] The Black Madonna of the Underworld wants to carry away the burdens that you are needlessly carrying, revitalize your embodied soul, and empower you to continue on her abundant labyrinth. Though we have been conditioned to hold it all, if we allow her, Black Madonna will swoop in to reverse our conditioning and return us to where we belong—cherished, held, guided, and invigorated by her ample, life-giving hands.

UNWINDING AND WINDING ON BLACK MADONNA'S LABYRINTH

The labyrinth promises us that we don't have to carry burdens that we were never meant to carry, that we can relinquish them to Black Madonna's capable hands and allow her to replace them with ease and joy. Those of us who have been chronically under-mothered are accustomed to accepting and even embracing burdens that were never meant for us, and we may be so accustomed to them that we do not even know that they are weighing us down and preventing us from receiving the ease and joy that Black Madonna offers. Our intentional labyrinth journey begins when we awaken to the incredible mothering hands of Black Madonna, who holds it all, and begin to release our burdens to her.

Preparing for the Practice

1. Find a labyrinth. If you know of a labyrinth near you, feel free to use that. However, over 6,600 labyrinths in more than 90 countries are registered at the Worldwide Labyrinth Locator (**labyrinthlocator.org**), an online database.[19] There's a good chance there's a labyrinth in your community, just waiting for you to discover it. If it's not accessible for you to physically go to a labyrinth, you can absolutely follow this practice in your sacred imagination. Simply use an image of a labyrinth and mentally walk its glorious path.

2. Prior to entering the labyrinth, set an intention for your walk. Your intention is entirely up to you. But one option is to identify a burden that you're carrying and set an intention to release it while you walk toward the center of the labyrinth. To deepen your embodiment, you can write your burden on a rock that you place at the center of the labyrinth. Or, if it's safe and feasible to do so, another invitation is to write your burden on a piece of paper that you burn at the center of the labyrinth.

The Practice

3. At the labyrinth entrance, take a moment for a few deep inhales
    and exhales. Then survey the entire labyrinth and imagine Our
    Lady of the Underworld holding it up with her large, life-giving
    hands. How does it feel to know that your entire journey is held
    and guided by her?

4. Begin walking the labyrinth's path at your own pace, taking as
    much time as you need to rest, pause, take deep breaths, and feel
    Black Madonna's presence. The labyrinth is an unwinding too—an
    unlearning, undoing, and releasing of what we need to be free of.
    If it's accessible to you, with each step you may want to take a
    deep breath and verbally repeat your intention, such as "I release
    ___________ to Black Madonna Who Holds It All So I Don't Have To."

5. When you arrive at the center of the labyrinth, feel free to stand,
    sit, lie down, or assume any position that feels good to your
    body. Mathematicians have confirmed that the center of the
    Chartres Labyrinth is the point of geometric perfect balance,
    often referred to as the "still point."[20] Take a moment to rest in
    Black Madonna's perfect balance, knowing that she wants to bring
    balance to your life by relieving you of the burdens that throw you
    off balance. When it feels good to you, release your burdens to
    Black Madonna. One option is to say a simple prayer, such as "I
    know you hold it all so I don't have to. I release __________ to you
    and receive your holy balance." If you brought a rock to leave at
    the center or have a paper burden to burn, feel free to do those
    embodied practices as well.

6. While you're still at the center, take a few moments to ask
    Black Madonna for a gift of abundance from her well of holy
    strong ones to carry forward on your journey. This gift could
    be an encouraging word or phrase, a profound sense of
    accompaniment, a piece of strategic wisdom, a sense of joy and
    ease, renewed trust, the appearance of a fluttering butterfly, a
    sweet whiff of summer rose, or a safe space to truly grieve and

the release that comes with a good grief session. What does
Black Madonna give you? How does it feel?

7. When you're ready, begin your walk out of the labyrinth, following
    the same path that brought you to the center. As you walk,
    you may want to set an intention to continue receiving Black
    Madonna's gift. You can do this by verbally or silently repeating
    "I receive your gift of __________ and carry it with me as I
    move through life." The practice of intentionally carrying Black
    Madonna's gift as we walk the labyrinth helps our bodies learn
    that even winding pathways are full of her gifts.

Integrating the Practice

8. Regina Renee Nyégbeh recommends the SIFT practice as a way
    to process and integrate a labyrinth experience. SIFT stands for
    Sensations, Images, Feelings, and Thoughts. So without judgment,
    take a few moments to reflect on your experience and notice
    any physical sensations, images, emotions, and thoughts. Do you
    notice any patterns? Do you notice any changes or shifts in your
    body, emotions, or mindset?

9. If you're anything like me, you may need to walk this labyrinth over
    and over and over again—and even release the same burden over
    and over and over again. This is not a nuisance to Black Madonna,
    for she loves to mother you.

5
INVOCATION

Black Madonna, our Great Defender,
Reveal yourself, display your love, unleash your power!
Exhausted, bombed out, bombarded—
We are under siege, chaos is rampant.
Our leaders, drunk with power,
Fascist fear coursing through their veins.
Politicians, pastors, parents, police—
Those charged to protect us stoke fires of unease.

Dutifully, we try to stay grounded,
We tune in to our breath.
But each new report of wartime atrocity,
climate calamity, lethal legislation,
Lands like a cannonball, explodes in our hearts.
In the midst of it all, we can't find our truth-roots,
Our peace veins, once robust, now run dry.
We need a new Source, one deeper, one wider.
Reveal yourself, display your love, unleash your power!

Cannonball-catching Queen of heaven and earth,
When all hope seems lost and our nerves cry out,
You valiantly emerge from the chaos,
You boldly rise from the ashes,
You fearlessly face off against the enemy,
You heroically halt missiles with your bare hands.
In one spectacular, unforgettable moment you
Reveal yourself, display your love, unleash your power!

Black Madonna, you are never exhausted,
Never bombed out, never bombarded.
Cosmic Multitasker, you juggle all the balls.
Your brazen right hand thwarts death, holds off enemy fire,
Your tender left hand nourishes life, draws
*   us close, lends your breast.*
Just one drop of your sacred milk
Banishes fear from our embodied souls.
A mere minute at your reassuring breast
Reinvigorates our veins with peace.

Resuscitated, reconnected, infused with
*   ancient yet timely wisdom—*
We now boldly proclaim what we know:
When our leaders betray us, God herself is our shield.
When our institutions fail us, God herself is our shield.
When chaos overwhelms, God herself is our shield.
When cannonballs launch, God herself is our shield.
When we feel most abandoned, God herself is our shield.
When all hope seems lost, God herself is our shield.

Black Madonna, our Great Defender,
Reveal yourself, display your love, unleash your power!
God herself is our shield.
God herself is our shield.
God herself is our shield.

Chapter 5

SHE FIERCELY DEFENDS US

Finding Refuge in Black Madonna's Cosmic Breast Milk

These days, our collective global reality feels like a battle scene in an *Avengers* movie. Chaos abounds. Amid the crumbling skyscrapers, piercing missiles, exploding cars, and stampeding crowds looking for cover, we instinctively know the cause of the destruction: Loki, the Norse god of chaos. Loki's entire strategy is to always begin by stirring up chaos because he understands that if he creates chaos, the resistance movement will be too distracted and divided to effectively fight back. So Loki attacks from every direction and with every weapon in his arsenal and power at his disposal—such as bombs, natural disasters, evil accomplices, deception—to rain chaos on earth and disarm the opposition.

Those of us who live in the United States are experiencing a real-life Loki attack. As I write this chapter, I am witnessing the United States of America, a country supposedly founded on democracy, descend into a dictatorship. Each day we are bombarded with a deluge of debilitating news reports of Donald Trump signing one oppressive (and often unconstitutional) executive order after another. The eyewitness accounts of unlawful deportations, brazen abuses of executive power, and piercing violations of human rights get exponentially worse as they reveal a well-laid plan to dismantle the U.S. Constitution and disrupt the balance of power that our society has long relied upon.

These are urgent times, disillusioning times, indescribable times.

Each report feels like yet another flying cannonball that detonates in our hearts and communities. Legal and media analysts call this bombardment tactic "flooding the zone" and its goal is to incite chaos by overwhelming people with so much scary and disheartening news that it literally creates a public frenzy. Taking his cues from patriarchy's playbook, Trump's hope is that we devote so much of our time, energy, and attention to reacting to the chaos—reading the latest report, freaking out, and obsessing over him—that we are too exhausted and dysregulated to effectively organize against him. This is not a new tactic: as Toni Morrison said long ago, "The function, the very serious function, of racism is distraction."[1] But it's an extremely effective tactic because we are survival-oriented beings; if we are being attacked, our instinct is to focus on and respond to the immediate threat. When the sky starts raining bombs, it's only natural that we run, duck, and cover in panic!

Though we try to stay grounded, our chaotic and vigilant nervous systems understand that we are under siege. Our breathing feels shallow, and our shoulders stand at high alert as Trump and his cronies launch a fascist regime while devastating physical and social wildfires rage. The ideologies, institutions, and norms that we used to rely on are long gone—relics of a prewar era. Our collective village is decimated, a dystopian wasteland leveled by a strategic onslaught of cannonballs called hopelessness, oligarchy, settler colonialism, resource scarcity, toxic masculinity, environmental racism, individualism, and Christian nationalism.

And that's just in the United States.

Around the world, genocides continue, nuclear threat looms, extreme poverty and exploitation thrive, and the global community crumbles under the weight of relentless polycrisis.

Can you feel your heart quicken? Your neck and jaw tense? Your pelvic floor muscles constrict as if your body must hold itself in because it can no longer trust the stable ground beneath it?

Our gloriously fallible humanity is on spectacular display as our nervous systems remain on high alert while we dodge cannonballs and wrestle with what to *feel*, much less what to *do*.

COPING WITH DIVINE ABANDONMENT

The chaos stirs up hopelessness, fear, self-destructive rage, and an every-man-for-himself impulse that separates us from the very people who can resist alongside us. And if you're anything like me, the chaos may also stir up feelings of divine abandonment. You see, I was taught that God was in the good, the light, the order, and the certainty. I was taught that God was present and active when my life was going well. But I wasn't taught that God was also present and active in the murky gray area, the darkness, the chaos, and the uncertainty. In fact, when my life wasn't going well, I was implicitly taught that God was not only absent but had intentionally abandoned me. Oft-repeated Bible verses like "Children, obey your parents as the Lord wants . . . then everything will be well with you and you will live a long life on the earth" (Ephesians 6:1–3) nurtured a vision of an exacting patriarchal god who only offered me a good life if I perfectly followed his commands. Consequently, whenever my life didn't go well, I believed that I had fallen from grace and somehow needed to repent or improve myself in order to regain access to the patriarchal god's tiny, terrifying circle of embrace.

Beyond individual pain, feelings of divine abandonment are often heightened when we encounter systemic pain—when oppressive forces such as colonialism, Islamophobia, and environmental racism launch cannonballs at entire segments of the population. Many of us didn't grow up with a divine being who actually gave a shit about colonialism, Islamophobia, or environmental racism. On the contrary, many of us grew up with gods who were entirely silent and absent when "bad things happened to good people." Or worse, some of us grew up with gods who seemed to be the source of systemic pain and suffering, as in the well-known Judeo-Christian story of Noah and the flood in which a petulant "God" murdered the entire global population simply because people didn't follow his commands. As a result, it's only natural that in the midst of systemic oppression, we automatically assume that we are all alone, that the Divine has abandoned us and is maybe even *against* us. During times of great pain, it can feel impossible to simply imagine, much less embrace the idea that the Divine is not only lovingly present but is actively standing with us and fighting for us.

If you find yourself vacillating between obsessive panic on the one hand and numbing hopelessness on the other—*you are not alone.*

If you are feeling exhausted, bombed out, and bombarded—*you are not alone.*

If you are feeling abandoned by the Divine—*you are not alone.*

The belief that God has abandoned us only pours gasoline on the fire of chaos. When we believe that God has abandoned us—or worse, is the evil source behind the chaos—we stop looking for divine intervention. When we stop looking for divine intervention, we become even more susceptible to hopelessness, fear, self-destructive rage, and hyper-individualism.

Even if we consciously believe in the trauma-informed, pro-liberation Black Madonna that we explored in Chapter 2, our bodies may not *feel* it. Research from the field of epigenetics teaches us that our cellular memory carries the beliefs and practices of our ancestors. In other words, if your ancestors practiced a white patriarchal religion with a scary, distant, hierarchical, punitive god—there's a good chance that your cells still carry white patriarchal religion in their memory. Despite our conscious rejection of a white patriarchal god, our unconscious often defaults to this god, especially in times of duress. In this way, our cellular memory has the power to tether us to our ancestors' spiritual impulses. So part of our work is uncovering noxious ancestral impulses and restoring life-giving spiritual impulses that enable us to connect with the abundance we long for.

This is one of many reasons why Black Madonna is such a soothing, restorative, and empowering vision of the Divine. Across eras, peoples, and faith traditions, our ancient Black Madonna has repeatedly revealed herself as the divine being who stands with and for her people, especially in the midst of antagonistic chaos. When chaos arises and the patriarchal god makes himself scarce, Black Madonna does the opposite: She comes running toward us, ready to fight on our behalf. In fact, writer Hettienne Grobler calls Black Madonna "the Mother of Chaos," in part because chaos doesn't scare, distract, or overwhelm her. As the ancient Sacred Black Feminine who emerged from the primordial darkness, Black Madonna knows how to navigate her way through a chaotic and uncertain situation. Rather than abandoning us in the chaos, Black Madonna mothers us in the chaos.

A BATTLE-READY QUEEN

At a time when white patriarchy wants to distract us with its big cannons, send us into a frantic tizzy, and convince us that we are all alone, Black Madonna rises from the ashes. But in a storm, Black Madonna offers more than soothing lullabies. In addition to nurturing us, Black Madonna is a fierce and battle-ready protector. If we heed her call, the stories of her fierce protection can fortify our spiritual imaginations and offer us the medicine that we need today. Though all of the 450-plus Black Madonnas around the world are revered for their solidarity with the most marginalized, the Black Madonna of Hal (Belgium) offers us a particularly vivid image of a divine being who refuses to abandon us in the midst of chaos.

The most ancient and popular statue of the Virgin Mary in the country of Belgium, the Black Madonna of Hal dates to the 13th century. (But much like many other Black Madonnas, she is a Christianized version of the much older Egyptian goddess Isis.) This heroic Black Madonna is credited with numerous miracles and life-saving interventions, but one especially stands out.

In the late 1500s, in the aftermath of the Protestant Reformation, Belgium remained a hotly contested battleground country as Protestants and Catholics fought to maintain control of the country. In the midst of war, the Protestants laid siege on the small village of Hal, which was prime spiritual real estate because it contained the Black Madonna of Hal, the most powerful and famous Virgin Mary shrine in the country. As is the case with most power struggles, it was the people, particularly those on the margins, who suffered the most. In 1580 the people of Hal were bombarded with hundreds of cannonballs as the Protestants attempted to take control of the village and its powerful Black Madonna shrine. The people of Hal were not mercenaries or soldiers; they were simple villagers who loved their Black Madonna and did not stand a chance against the Protestant militia. Terrified, the people of Hal frantically raced in every direction, trying to outrun their impending demise.

With cannonballs dropping like lethal raindrops, all hope seemed lost.

But, as the story goes, Black Madonna exited the church at the center of town, made her way to the city walls, and courageously stood atop the ramparts, facing off against the Protestant army. Standing tall and with her voluminous robe flowing in the wind, she caught dozens of cannonballs with her bare hands and rerouted the remaining cannonballs to evacuated areas of the village. As the people ran in hopeless terror, Black Madonna stood at the helm, catching the heat and saving the village from destruction. The Black Madonna of Hal is so revered for this epic miracle that she is often depicted with cannonballs at the foot of her statue, as you can see in antique and vintage images.

When the people thought that they were divinely abandoned, God herself became their shield.

When the chaos overwhelmed the people, God herself appeared and stood with them in the chaos.

When the bombs were too much for the people to handle, God herself handled them.

THE CURIOUS CASE OF THE COSMIC BREAST MILK

In many battle scenes in the *Avengers* movies, there's a pivotal turning point. Just when Loki is about to claim victory and all hope for humanity seems lost, the Avengers appear and begin to fight alongside the citizens of earth. Hope is reborn! Suddenly, people stop frantically running because they see that they are no longer alone. Suddenly, people who were scared shitless become courageous warriors as they fight alongside the Avengers. Suddenly, the chaos doesn't seem overwhelming because the people know that the Avengers are helping them navigate the chaos.

When we know that God is with us in the chaos, everything changes. We can stop aimlessly and frantically running from the chaos and from each other because we now know that God herself is catching cannonballs with her bare hands. We no longer need to panic because we know we are not abandoned. Instead, we can take a deep breath, pause, and remember what we know to be true. We can take a deep breath, pause, and remember that the chaos is designed to knock us off our truth-roots and distract us from the sacred work to which we are called. We can take a deep breath, pause, and remember our natural gifts so we can begin to use them for freedom. When we know that God is with us in the chaos, we can take a deep breath, pause, and remember.

But practically speaking, how do we remember that God herself is with us in the chaos? Chaos is designed to knock us off our truth-roots, to make us forget *who* we are and *whose* we are. How do we remember the truth even while cannonballs rain down around us?

Here, we can turn again to the Black Madonna of Hal to show us the way—for her very statue lovingly shows us *how* to surrender to her, no matter what is going on around us. The Black Madonna of Hal is incredibly unique in that she is a *virgo lactans*, a nursing Madonna. Yes, the same Black Madonna who stood upon the city ramparts and caught cannonballs with her bare hands did it while simultaneously breastfeeding her child. The Black Madonna of Hal is a Cosmic Multitasker, a divine archetype that truly *can* juggle all the balls. Most Marian statues in general and Black Madonna statues in particular depict a prim, proper, and fully clothed Mary holding a toddler-aged child in her arms or on her lap. Nothing scandalous to see here. But the extremely rare virgo lactans depict Mary with at least one breast fully exposed and actively breastfeeding an infant child. Gasp!

Though virgo lactans are rare now, they were quite common for much of Christianity, and were often the primary way that early devotees experienced and understood Mary. In fact, many historians believe that the earliest surviving image of Mary is a 2nd-century fresco painting discovered in the Catacomb of Priscilla in Rome. In the image, which is painted on subterranean rock, we encounter a tender and earthy Black Madonna nursing a Christ child.[2] Far from the fancy and queenly images of Black Madonna that we often see in cathedrals today, the intimate and deeply relatable Black Madonna in the Catacomb of Priscilla reminds us that, at her core, the Sacred Black Feminine is an Earth Mother who infinitely nourishes and tends to our very human needs. In late antiquity, this image and others like it were reproduced throughout the Christian world and Black Madonna devotees encountered it early and often, thus shaping their experience of her as a tender and relatable mother who is a constant source of nourishment and care.

But Black Madonna isn't just any mother, so of course her breast milk isn't just any breast milk. She is both Earth Mother *and* Queen of the Cosmos, and Black Madonna's nourishing breast milk isn't limited to the physical world. Since the advent of Christianity, devotees have believed that Mary's breast milk possesses special powers. For example, one of the most frequented pilgrimage destinations in the Holy Land is the Chapel of the Milk Grotto in Bethlehem, a monument to what is perhaps Mary's first "breast milk miracle." According to the story, shortly after Jesus's birth, a few drops of Mary's milk fell onto the rock floor of an ancient grotto and immediately transformed the rock color from pink to white. Since then, the floor has possessed healing properties—and birth parents who are having difficulty conceiving or breastfeeding have traveled to the grotto, touched the miraculous floor, and been healed. By the 5th century, the grotto was so frequented that the existing chapel was built to house it. It's impossible to count how many miracles have occurred there over the centuries—but from just 2000 to 2003, the priest and caretaker of the chapel received 170 reports of miraculous conceptions.[3] To this day, the chapel continues to receive numerous letters of gratitude from once-infertile birth parents who miraculously conceived after their pilgrimage to the grotto.[4]

Beyond physical healing powers, Black Madonna's breast milk also possesses protective powers. Historian Cecilia Dorger, who has devoted her career to the study of virgo lactans, confirms that into the late medieval and Renaissance periods, devotees believed that Black Madonna's breast milk possessed mystical qualities that could protect them from impending doom. For example, Bernard of Cluny, a 12th-century French monk and poet, often "praised Mary's breasts and the milk that flows from them for their ability to defeat and weaken the savage enemy and thereby save us."[5] In other words, Black Madonna's cosmic breast milk is a source of protection to those who drink it. This historical insight helps us more fully appreciate the awe-inspiring image of the Black Madonna of Hal, who catches cannonballs with one hand while simultaneously breastfeeding with the other. To devotees like Bernard of Cluny, the Black Madonna of

Hal's stance as a virgo lactans empowered rather than impeded her ability to catch cannonballs with her bare hands. Her breastfeeding and cannonball catching were one and the same, simply two sides of the same protective coin. When these devotees found themselves in desperate need of protection, they "ingested her cosmic breast milk" by looking to her first for protection and seeking her wise guidance as they navigated the cannonballs of their lives.

In fact, St. Bernard of Clairvaux, another 12th-century French monk and arguably the most influential champion of Black Madonna, is said to have received his world-renowned wisdom directly from Black Madonna's breast milk. While a young student, Bernard stood before the Black Madonna of Châtillon-sur-Seine (France) and asked her to reveal herself as a mother. At that moment, the statue came to life and several drops of breast milk squirted into Bernard's mouth.[6] From that time on, Bernard was infused with cosmic wisdom and began preaching extensively about Black Madonna and urging devotees to reclaim divine feminine aspects of Christian theology such as an embrace of the physical body and a love for the natural world.

His writings and impact were so great that they incited a Marian renaissance within Christianity that even impacted the sacred architecture. Prior to the 12th-century Marian renaissance, in which Mary's divinity and feminine attributes were reclaimed and celebrated, many European houses of worship were built in the hypermasculine, fortress-like Romanesque architectural tradition. But as the Marian renaissance flourished, a new, much more feminine architectural style emerged, and communities began building ornate, lace-like Gothic cathedrals inspired by their devotion to Mary's divine femininity and expressly dedicated to her.

Shortly after his death, St. Bernard was named an official saint in record time and was also granted the intellectual distinction of being named a "Marian Doctor of the Church."[7] Due in large part to Bernard of Clairvaux's influence, images of virgo lactans remained popular through the Middle Ages and into the Renaissance period. A wonderful devotional resource, the virgo lactans helped devotees connect with both Black Madonna's earthy and relatable body and her cosmic powers, and helped them remember to call on her first when they needed protection and wisdom.

However, the printing press changed everything. The advent of the printing press coincided with an abundance of easily accessible pornography that encouraged the sexualization of women's bodies, as well as wider circulation of anatomical drawings for medical purposes that demystified the body. According to historian David Gibson, "Both undermined traditional views of the body as a reflection of the divine" and diminished the popularity of virgo lactans as a devotional resource. But patriarchy dealt the final blow to the virgo lactans. Gibson explains, "The mass-marketing of the Bible and the rise of Protestantism . . . encouraged a focus on the text of the Scriptures and discouraged the use of images and Catholic practices like devotion to the Virgin Mary and the saints. The cultural shift was so great that even Catholics soon came to regard the breast as an inappropriate image for churches. Instead, the sacrifice of the cross, the suffering Jesus, became the dominant motif of Christianity while the Nativity was sanitized into a Hallmark card."[8] The patriarchal urges to promote a mind that is detached from the body, embrace certainty and resist mystery, elevate the written word over art, and silence the divine feminine ultimately produced a religious culture that banished the powerful and liberating image of the virgo lactans. Today, as far as I know, there are only three surviving Black Madonna virgo lactans: the Black Madonna of Hal, the Black Madonna of Nazare (Portugal), and the Mother of God of the Milk (Spain).

Because this potent, intimate, and life-giving image has been all but erased from our collective spiritual memory, it is easy for us to forget that Black Madonna is an endless source of spiritual nourishment, wisdom, and protection. But now more than ever, our anti-nurturing and patriarchal world needs a divine archetype that nourishes rather than chastises, communicates rather than dominates, leans in closer when we are in distress, and promises that if we drink of her cosmic breast milk, we will embody the courage and wisdom we need to collaborate with her as she restores the world. In other words, we need to follow in Bernard of Clairvaux's footsteps and usher in a Black Madonna renaissance—a Black Madonnaissance, if you will. Bernard began by first seeking and drinking Black Madonna's breast milk. That's where we can start too.

OUR LADY OF THE SOFT SPACE BETWEEN A ROCK AND A HARD PLACE

The stories about the Black Madonna of Hal help us experience Black Madonna as both a fierce military defender and a nurturing mother. As the ancient Sacred Black Feminine who has seen it all and survived it all, Black Madonna can easily establish a sacred refuge and defend and nourish her people, even in the harshest situations. So it's not surprising that many Black Madonnas live in sanctuaries that are built into massive rock formations that are rather inhospitable to green growth. One famous example is the 12th-century Black Madonna of Montserrat (Spain) who presides over a multi-peak mountain range also named Montserrat, which means "jagged rock." The mountain range, which rises from barren and even somewhat harsh terrain, lives up to its formidable name. Though Black Madonna's monastery is massive, it is almost overshadowed by the bulging limestone outcrops that surround it and the phallus-shaped peaks that tower above.

Almost. It turns out that no jagged mountain range is more formidable than Black Madonna's abundance.

You see, the first thing I noticed when I visited Montserrat was how peaceful it was. Despite the crowds of pilgrims and the hot, howling wind whipping around the mountain, as soon as I stepped across the threshold of the monastery, I was engulfed in a trance-like wave of peace. My labored breathing and heart rate instantly slowed to a resting state even though I had just hiked up a mountain en route to Black Madonna. My inner highway, which is usually buzzing and zipping with thoughts, came to a standstill, and my conscious attention was enraptured by Black Madonna's infinitely welcoming invitation to come experience the life that she offers even in the midst of the most inhospitable terrain.

Amid a literal "hard place," I found deep solace and watched in awe as hundreds of pilgrims experienced similar peace in the presence of this Black Madonna, who is seated in the Throne of Wisdom posture, a formidable "power position"—upper body erect, head held high, shoulders rolled back, feet planted firmly on the ground—as if she is squaring off against the entire world in defense of her people. The Throne of Wisdom position is so structured and fierce that

Black Madonna's body itself resembles a throne, mystically affirming that her sacred feminine body is so full of divine wisdom that she is both the essence of wisdom *and* the throne on which wisdom is seated. As the Mother of Abundance from whom all life emanates, Black Madonna is both the birther and carrier of all things, including wisdom. Clarissa Pinkola Estés calls Black Madonna the "Source without source." Black Madonna is the Life that births life and the Wisdom that births wisdom—in herself and in us. Even more, her throne of wisdom is so expansive and generative that she is able to hold all aspects of life within it, including herself. Eastern Orthodox Christians, who since the 5th century have called Black Madonna the "Container of the God Whom Nothing Can Contain," have been extolling this wonderful mystery for centuries.

Any Black Madonna who is seated in the Throne of Wisdom position is a force to be reckoned with, so it's not surprising that many Black Madonnas are seated this way. But the Throne of Wisdom posture is much more common among the 12th-century French Black Madonnas and rather rare among the Spanish ones, who are typically standing up. So the fact that the Black Madonna of Monsterrat is seated in this position further underscores her exceptional power that can never be overshadowed by a phallic mountain range. And yet, the Black Madonna of Montserrat's alluring facial expression, with its relaxed jawline and slight, Mona Lisa–like smile, beautifully balances her fierce posture and showcases the truth that she is both a powerhouse and an attentive Mother of Abundance. Though her formidable posture affirms her status as powerful Black Madonna who presides over a literal jagged mountain range, her smile beckons each of us and assures us that all are welcome to join her on her expansive, wide, wise, unconditionally hospitable lap.

My nickname for the Black Madonna of Montserrat is Our Lady of the Soft Space Between a Rock and a Hard Place because since the medieval era, people have called on her when they are in extreme crisis and really need a loving and wise liberator. As the Throne of Wisdom, she is as cunning as she is fierce. So it's not surprising that she is also known for navigating especially complex and political situations and for protecting her people in the most subversive and creative ways, as the following story reveals.

In the 1600s, a distinguished abbess (think: Head-Nun-in-Charge) at a Spanish monastery did the illegal and "unthinkable": she got pregnant.[9] This was during the height of the Spanish Inquisition, a punitive and patriarchal power grab disguised as piety. Not surprisingly, when the Church patriarchy discovered that one of its most influential nuns was pregnant, they sent word that they were coming to put her on trial and uphold the law (think: kangaroo court and lynch mob). At this point, the abbess was as good as dead—for controlling women's bodies was critical to upholding the patriarchy, and they needed to make a spectacle of her in order to fearmonger other women into submission. The story doesn't include any details on how the abbess became pregnant, such as whether it was by force or consent. But regardless of the circumstances that led to the pregnancy, given the violent and misogynistic legalism of the medieval Catholic Church, I imagine this nun was scared shitless.

According to the legend, before the Spanish Inquisitors could journey to the remote monastery, the abbess and her nun friends called out to the Black Madonna of Montserrat for help. She was already widely known for helping people get out of the worst situations—and though the nuns had no idea how Black Madonna would deliver their beloved leader, they knew they could put their hope in her. Not surprisingly, Black Madonna instantly appeared to the abbess. But rather than simply comfort her, the imminently practical Mother of Abundance safely induced and delivered the nun's premature baby and took the baby to a nearby family who could love it as their own. Then, the politically savvy Black Madonna returned to the abbess and miraculously sewed her up so that when the patriarchal lynch mob arrived the following day and examined the abbess's body, they found her to be a virgin!

Our Lady of the Soft Space Between a Rock and a Hard Place knows a thing or two about carving out soft spaces within a harsh and rocky political and spiritual landscape because she's been generating life-giving peace amid a barren and rugged mountain range for centuries. Even more, as the ageless Sacred Black Feminine who has participated in the human story since she birthed humans, this isn't her first rodeo in general and this definitely isn't her first rodeo when it comes to the particular predicament of premarital pregnancy. As you may recall, within the Christian tradition, Black Madonna appears as Mary the mother of Jesus. This is the same Mary who, as a betrothed teenager, found herself pregnant. So of course Black Madonna could be counted on to empathize rather than condemn the pregnant abbess. Of course Black Madonna, the mother of arguably the most polarizing political figure in human history, knew how to navigate a complex political situation. Of course Black Madonna, who was once a young pregnant Palestinian teenager whose body was prodded and probed by patriarchal men, knew to anticipate and effectively outwit the patriarchal men who physically prodded and probed the abbess's body. Of course Black Madonna—who at the ghastly, lynch mob–fueled crucifixion of her own son, lovingly agreed to adopt his disciple John as her son—understood that the sacred act of mothering is not biologically based. Rather, it is a sacred act of community love.

Of course.

Of course.

Of course.

Black Madonna is the Source without source, the Wisdom *and* the birther of wisdom, and the Container of the God Whom Nothing Can Contain.

With her, there are no first rodeos. Only an abundant chorus of *of courses*.

REACHING FOR HER "MILKIES"

My home is basically a Black-art-infused carnival. Stripes and polka dots cover the windows and floors, bold primary colors beam from every corner, and eye-catching art depicting Black joy and Black audacity cover the walls. So when my adopted nephew, Malcolm, visited me for a week last summer along with his family, I wasn't surprised when he immediately began exploring my home with wide-eyed wonder. But I was unsure of how he would experience the unique Black art above my bed: three watercolor nude portraits of me. I almost removed the images before Malcolm's family arrived because, like the Renaissance-era patriarchs who banished the virgo lactans, I wasn't sure if it was appropriate for my young niblings to be exposed to nude images of me, even though they are art. But Malcolm's parents assured me that the portraits were fine to display because they were teaching their children that bodies are meant to be celebrated—not feared or commodified. So I heeded their advice and kept the portraits on my wall, all the while wondering what reaction, if any, my niblings would have to my portraits. But I couldn't have predicted Malcolm's response.

As soon as he wandered into my room, Malcolm's eyes landed on my portraits. Within a split second, he sprinted toward my bed, leapt onto it, and scrambled toward the nude portraits while gleefully shouting, "*Milkies! Milkies! Auntie Neena has milkies!*"

Mesmerized, Malcolm sat cross-legged on the bed, his body in a meditative stillness except for his head, which rapidly alternated between looking at me and looking at my exposed breasts in the portraits. I knew what was coming next.

"Auntie Neena, can I have some milk from your milkies?" Malcolm inquired.

"Auntie Neena doesn't have any milk in her milkies," I awkwardly responded in the third person. "But I can snuggle with you, if you'd like."

You see, I understood why Malcolm, a four-year-old who no longer subsists on breast milk, still desperately craves it. Though he now ingests "big boy food," Malcolm still breastfeeds for a few minutes every morning because it fosters the intimate connection he hungers for. He no longer relies on breastfeeding for physical sustenance, but he absolutely still relies on it for social sustenance. I knew that even though I couldn't offer him breastmilk, I could offer him the social equivalent: a good ol'-fashioned, wholesome snuggle session with Auntie Neena.

To Malcolm, breast milk is love.

Breast milk is protection.

Breast milk is accompaniment.

Breast milk is embrace.

Breast milk is guidance.

Those few minutes of breastfeeding in the morning remind Malcolm that even though his mommy, Leah, now devotes most of her breast milk to his two younger siblings, she is still deeply devoted to him, connected to him, and attentive to him. Those few minutes of breastfeeding in the morning help Malcolm remain *psychically* dependent on his mommy even though he is becoming more and more *physically* independent. Those few minutes of breastfeeding in the morning empower Malcolm to boldly move through his world with the assurance that his mommy is close by and ready to come to his rescue, should he need her. To Malcolm, breast milk is the nectar of secure attachment.

Children are often the most inspiring mystics. Especially during times of anguish, children seek the nourishing and protective comfort of the breast. The fact that Malcolm immediately zeroed in on my "milkies" teaches us that the medicine we most need during times of distress can be found in Black Madonna's breast milk, if only we reach for it. In fact, times of duress—when our patriarchal conditioning stirs up feelings of hopelessness, divine abandonment, and overwhelm— are the ideal times for us to rewire our spiritual DNA by actively seeking Black Madonna's cosmic breast milk. When the cannonballs are sailing toward us and the urge to succumb to chaos-induced panic is fierce, that is precisely when we can begin to understand, as Bernard of Cluny understood, the shielding powers of Black Madonna's cosmic breast milk. Times of duress give us the sacred opportunity to discover the magical truth that when we reach for her breast milk, we also summon her cannonball-catchin' protection. Times of duress help us powerfully reclaim the long-lost image of the virgo lactans and embody a relationship with the Divine that is grounded in protection, secure attachment, accompaniment, and empowerment.

Black Madonna has the power, experience, and wisdom to restore our world. She is perfectly equipped to help us implement the world we long for. She belongs to all of us—and as the cannonballs detonate all around us, she stands in the wasteland with us, reminding us that God herself has not forsaken us. She reminds us that the Sacred Black Feminine who has withstood the test of time continues to stand in solidarity with the most hopeless and marginalized today. A battle-ready queen, she invites us to surrender to her fierce protection and be empowered by her subversive life force.

FINDING REFUGE IN BLACK MADONNA'S COSMIC BREAST MILK

Black Madonna cherishes you and wants to protect you from the cannonballs that assault you. No matter the cannonballs in your life—be they climate crisis, genocide, anti-Blackness, the crumbling of stabilizing institutions like democracy, the tragic death of a loved one, chronic illness, transphobia, domestic abuse, housing insecurity, oppressive regimes, or any other challenges—Black Madonna wants to stand with you, shield you, help you navigate to safety, and empower you to join in her liberating work.

As the image and story of the Black Madonna of Hal teaches us, finding refuge in Black Madonna means seeking and receiving her breast milk. This simple, step-by-step practice involves naming the cannonballs that are whizzing around us, uncovering and naming the voice of our patriarchal religious conditioning, and actively inviting Black Madonna to shield and guide us by speaking her wisdom in our situation.

If we want Black Madonna to offer us her cosmic breast milk when we are threatened by the cannonballs, we need to explicitly invite her to guide and transform our inner spiritual landscape. As somatic practitioner Kelsey Blackwell teaches us in her book *Decolonizing the Body*, "The inner critic is loud, especially when we are afraid." During times of duress, our inner spiritual landscape is often dominated by an internalized patriarchal god who is an inner critic. Even those of us who consciously resist the notion of a patriarchal god often manifest one. This is only human; as Jungian analyst Selma Nemer details in her book *The Beheaded Goddess*, we live in such an anti-nurturing, patriarchal society that most of us manifest an internalized patriarchal god when we are under duress.

To a degree, all of us live with or have lived with an internalized patriarchal god simply because we have been conditioned by patriarchy, which seeks to shame and control people as a means of maintaining its power hierarchy. This god stirs up divine abandonment and hopelessness via the following:

- Embodied fear—the voice of fear, resource scarcity, and false beliefs of abandonment, and the urge to freeze/not act when we are distressed

- Embodied reactivity—the voice of reactivity and the urge to lash out/get defensive and/or numb with substances when we are distressed

- Embodied shame—the voice of shame and condemnation, and the urge to control ourselves and/or others when we are distressed

If your inner spiritual landscape seems like a smoldering, desolate, hopeless, and barren mess—you are not alone. This practice helps us intentionally infuse our inner spiritual landscape with her life-giving and life-saving powers. Her cosmic breast milk has the power to transform the fears, reactivity, and shame that we carry so that no matter what we are going through, our inner spiritual landscape is resourced and shielded by Black Madonna and is empowered to bloom.

1. *Name the cannonball.* Begin by identifying a situation about which you are currently experiencing distress. Literally anything that is producing or stimulating anxiety, doubt, fear, shame, a desire to numb your feelings, or any urge to avoid talking to others or the Divine about it or trusting others or the Divine with it.

2. *Face the cannonball.* Once you've identified the situation, allow yourself to just be present to the situation for three to five minutes. One way to do this is to simply describe the situation to yourself (the who, what, and where, for example) or envision the situation in your mind and allow it to live in your body.

3. *Ask your internalized patriarchal god to speak.* It might be counterintuitive or even terrifying to give voice to this god. But the internalized patriarchal god often works outside of our conscious awareness and maintains control by flying under the radar in the form of our embodied fear, embodied reactivity, and embodied shame. In this way, he also launches cannonballs at us, even when we are already under fire. When we consciously confront his cannonballs (e.g., his voice and urges), we allow Black Madonna to shield us from them too. So we're going to intentionally hand the mic to the internalized patriarchal god, give him a chance to speak his "truth," and trust that cannonball-

catchin' Black Madonna will shield us from overwhelm. To that end, follow these steps:

a. Set a timer for three to five minutes and ask your embodied fear (the voice of fear, resource scarcity, and false beliefs of abandonment, and the urge to freeze/not act when you are distressed) to speak its truth. Write down or record whatever your embodied fear has to say.

b. Take a *deep*, full-body breath.

c. Next, set a timer again for three to five minutes and ask your embodied reactivity (the voice of reactivity, and the urge to lash out/get defensive and/or numb with substances when you are distressed) to speak its truth. Write down or record whatever your embodied reactivity has to say.

d. Take a *deep*, full-body breath.

e. Next, set a timer again for three to five minutes and ask your embodied shame (the voice of shame and condemnation, and the urge to control ourselves and/or others when we are distressed) to speak its truth. Write down or record whatever your embodied shame has to say.

f. Take a *deep*, full-body breath.

4. *Reach for Black Madonna's cosmic breast milk.* As the cannonball-catchin' Queen of the Universe as well as the Earth Mother who offers cosmic breast milk, Black Madonna is truly the most qualified to speak to your situation. So invite her to speak into the situation as well.

a. Set a timer again for three to five minutes and allow Black Madonna (the voice of unconditional love, accompaniment, and wisdom) to speak her truth. Black Madonna can speak broadly to the situation and/or specifically to your embodied fear, embodied reactivity, and/or embodied shame. Write down or record whatever Black Madonna has to say. Here are a few tips:

- It may be difficult for you to access Black Madonna, especially when you're in distress. When this happens to me, I imagine a loving teacher or friend and ask myself, "What would they say to me about this situation?" This helps me access the essence of Black Madonna's voice without shaming myself for not being able to access Black Madonna on demand.

- If a particular Black Madonna feels especially resonant in this moment (e.g., the Black Madonna of Charity/Ọṣun/the Black Madonna of Love or the Black Madonna of Paris/"Our Lady of Fuck Around and Find Out"), feel free to imagine her in a specific way. But it's okay if no particular Black Madonna comes to mind. You can simply imagine Black Madonna more generally.

- If you're having trouble connecting with Black Madonna, it can be helpful to do this part with an image of Black Madonna in sight. Allow the image to bring her words into your consciousness. What do you notice about her features? How might they give insight into how she is speaking to this situation and to your internalized patriarchal god? What do you notice about her surroundings? How might they give insight into how she is speaking to this situation and to your internalized patriarchal god? What do you notice about your emotions and body sensations as you look at this image? How might they give insight into how she is speaking to this situation and to your internalized patriarchal god?

b. Take a *deep*, full-body breath.

5. *Rest and reflect.* Finally, take a few moments to engage in the simple practice of noticing. Noticing helps us connect our thoughts and emotions with our bodily sensations and behaviors. The more we understand these connections, the better we are able to transform them.

a.   What did it feel like to literally allow your internalized patriarchal god to speak?

b.   What did it feel like to literally invite Black Madonna to speak?

c.   Did you notice any changes in your beliefs or emotions after you completed the practice? Do any of the beliefs seem more or less true to you now?

d.   Compared to when you were allowing your embodied fear, embodied reactivity, or embodied shame to speak, how did your body feel while inviting Black Madonna to speak? Did you notice a difference in your bodily sensations? Some polar sensations to consider: tightness/looseness, numbness/sensitivity, warm/cold, constricted/expansive, slouched/erect, anxious/calm, flighty/grounded.

e.   If it feels life-giving to you, take a moment to thank Black Madonna for her life-giving and life-saving breast milk and for supporting your healing journey.

6
INVOCATION

Mother of mystics and monks, weirdos and wanderers,
We are burned-out believers, awakening
*   and longing for renewal.*
We hoped that light and certainty would make us whole.
Yes, we made offerings, served faithfully,
*   abided by the Good Book.*
But the church's bright lights and clamor of creeds,
Which promised fulfillment and a clear path to Heaven,
Have left us disillusioned and agonized by a spiritual migraine.
Woo our souls into your dark forest,
*   where we can be born again.*

Zealous Blaze, Momma Volcano,
In your ominous forest, you reign over fire and lava;
Even the most powerful, cunning, and sinister forces
Cannot decimate what you have willed to live.
Yes, you gather the flames that are meant to harm
And transform them into holy, molten fire that burns
Burns, burns away all that stifles true life.
When the fires of this world are set to destroy us,
Woo our souls into your dark forest,
*   where we can be born again.*

Cosmic Womb, even amid senseless pain,
You liberate us from the need to know control,
To see beyond our next step.
In your forest womb, you quiet our senses

And we become fetuses again, free to depend.
As we rest in you, your sacred umbilical cord feeds us
A feast of peace that passes all understanding.
Woo our souls into your dark forest,
where we can be born again.

Chapter 6

SHE SOOTHES OUR DEEPEST WOUNDS

Transforming Pain into Power in Black Madonna's Ominously Dark Forest

I've never been trick-or-treating. My conservative Christian parents didn't allow us to attend school on Halloween, much less celebrate the holiday by trick-or-treating. (To Mom's credit, on Halloween she always took us on a family field trip to the Hershey's chocolate factory, where we could sample sweets to our hearts' content. My mom is not a fool!)

During the evening, instead of trick-or-treating among the "dark" forces "out there" in our neighborhood, we went to our church's Hallelujah party, which was a "sacred," light-filled haven. The Hallelujah party was basically a Halloween party; we dressed up in costumes, filled our pillowcases with candy, and bobbed for apples. The only major difference is that our church's Hallelujah party instilled in me the dualistic idea that darkness is always equated with evil and the absence of God.

With only one exception, every corner of the Hallelujah party was bathed in shimmering light. Even though it was almost daylight saving time and the sun set early, the floodlights the church rented made it seem like daylight in the s expansive courtyard. The only section of the party that was shrouded in darkness was the make-believe Hell. Yes, there was a Hell at the Hallelujah party. The Heaven-and-Hell immersive experience, the church version of a haunted house, was the centerpiece of the party. Each group of friends was paired with an attendant who led us through intricate worlds populated by actors who played celestial beings or demons. First, our attendant gently guided us into Heaven, where we listened to the cherubic choir sing, were warmly greeted by angels, gorged ourselves on sugary angel food cake, marveled at all the twinkle lights and glitter, reveled in the positive vibes and glee, easefully sauntered down a clear, flower-lined path—and, yes, finally met Jesus.

Then our attendant forcefully steered us into Hell, which was entirely dark except for a creepy red-hued black light and intermittent, unpredictable flashes of strobe light that were designed to startle. There we witnessed enchained people crying out as they were mercilessly beaten by growling demons against an aural backdrop of screeching, anarchic heavy metal music. After experiencing the expansive and light-filled Heaven, Hell had a claustrophobic feel—not because it was physically small but because the chaotic darkness produced a cruel maze in which every turn was a wrong turn that simply led us deeper into the chaos. It was terrifying. As I shivered and shuddered in my pink tulle princess costume, I vowed to do whatever it took to avoid Hell.

In Heaven, the lights were bright and all the people—the choir, the angels, and Jesus—were white. In Hell, the lights were dim and all the people—both the damned and the demons—were Black.

The not-so-subtle message: God is white and dwells in light, order, joy, and an easy, clear path. Even more, God is definitively *not* Black and is fully absent in darkness, chaos, pain, and disillusionment.

In this way, I was inducted into Christianity's impoverished spirituality of darkness: a spirituality that left little room for me to affirm the divinity of Black people like myself or trust that God was holding me close even when life was clouded by disappointment and disillusionment.

When we associate light with the presence of the Divine, we automatically associate darkness with the absence of the Divine. So if we're experiencing darkness of any sort—be it personal and/or societal, physical and/or spiritual—we tend to think that God is far, far away. Among other things, the antagonistic relationship between darkness and the Divine is a pitfall of dualism. Because we see light and darkness as opposite ends of a spectrum, it is difficult for us to imagine a divine being that exists, thrives, and radiates at all points on the spectrum. It is even more difficult for us to imagine a *Black* divine being that embodies the darkness, lovingly carries us through darkness, and even redemptively births beauty in the darkness.

Contrary to what white patriarchy may have taught us, Black Madonna's Black skin powerfully proclaims that darkness is divine and invites us to seek the Divine in the midst of darkness. As the ancient Sacred Black Feminine who crosses oceans in pursuit of us, Black Madonna is perpetually looking for ways for us to grow deeper and deeper in union with her and to receive her love no matter what we are going through—including chaos, pain, and disillusionment. She knows that our impoverished spirituality of darkness impedes our ability to experience her, much less seek her, in the midst of chaos and pain. Thankfully, Black Madonna, full of grace and illuminated by her radiantly dark skin, is out with lanterns looking for us. Her shimmering Black skin dispels white patriarchy's notion that God is confined to whiteness and light and beckons us to draw near to her so she can strategically heal and nurture our impoverished spiritual imaginations.

THE BLACK MADONNA OF THE OMINOUSLY DARK FOREST

The Black Madonna of Einsiedeln lives deep in the Swiss alpine forest and has been powerfully nourishing and expanding pilgrims' spirituality of darkness since at least the 9th century. Unlike the white patriarchal god, she does not abandon or banish us in the darkness. Rather, she's a divine being who wonderfully embodies the ancient psalmist's declaration that "Even though I walk through the valley of the shadow of death, I will fear no evil. For you are with me" (Psalm 23:4).

Her official title is Our Lady of the Finsterwald, *finsterwald* being an illustrious German word meaning "obscure," "dark," "gloomy," and "somber forest." Finsterwalds are scary places, in part because they are unruly and unpredictable. In the finsterwald, you are at the mercy of the elements, fate, and the wildness of life; money, prestige, and the law and order of the city are not going to protect you. As Jungian analyst

Fred Gustafson writes, the finsterwald in which Black Madonna made her home over 1,000 years ago "was a place of uncertainties, of natural laws that could be either hazardous or beneficial to whomever entered it. It was characterized by its unpredictable nature—a nature that one could not manipulate and change according to will, but which one had to submit to by listening to, observing, adjusting, and ultimately respecting."[1] The Black Madonna of Einsiedeln lives there—at the epicenter of the unpredictable, chaotic, and ominously dark forest that cannot be manipulated or tamed. By planting her roots in such an ominously dark place, she calls to us and guides us as we untangle from the lies that God is absent in the darkness and reclaim and reweave the truth that she is fully present in the darkness.

Our Lady of the Ominously Dark Forest's legend begins with Meinrad, a young, multitalented monk who lived in Zurich in the early 800s. The community celebrated and cherished Meinrad as both an inspiring scholar and a personable pastor; not surprisingly, Meinrad would eventually be canonized as a Catholic saint. But young St. Meinrad began to long for more.

You see, much as it remains today, St. Meinrad's Zurich was an intellectual and commercial center. Throughout history, cities have been associated with light, the sun, and the patriarchal values of logic, linear thinking, and law and order. Within the monastery in Zurich, the patriarchal impulses of reason, tradition, and control ruled Meinrad's spiritual life. In the monastery God was found in the light, in certainty, in the predictability and control of a city and religion ruled by tradition and strict moral laws. Despite our vast racial, gender, and cultural differences, I feel a sweet kinship with St. Meinrad. I imagine that if his medieval Swiss spiritual community created an immersive Heaven-and-Hell, it would have been eerily similar to the one I experienced as a child.

St. Meinrad craved a more robust spirituality that made room for him to experience the Divine in the midst of chaos and adventure, and even in the pain and disillusionment that we experience when we can't control ourselves or the people and circumstances that surround us. So despite his growing popularity, St. Meinrad decided to leave the monastery in Zurich in order to live as a hermit. But before he left, Hildegard of Zurich, the abbess at the nearby convent, gifted him a wooden statue of the Virgin Mary. With the statue in his embrace, St. Meinrad embarked on a life of solitude. When he eventually settled in the alpine finsterwald about 25 miles from Zurich, only the statue, Our Lady of the Finsterwald, accompanied him into the chaotic darkness.

The finsterwald in which St. Meinrad built his little hermitage was full of bandits and thieves, wild animals, and the harsh environmental elements of the Swiss Alps. Many monks during St. Meinrad's time would likely have asserted that the Divine existed solely among the light and rational thinking that characterized the city and was conspicuously absent in the unruly finsterwald. But St. Meinrad knew differently. He knew that in order to experience the fullness of the Divine, he had to commune with her in the ominously dark forest and surrender to her guidance and protection in the midst of the chaos—without trying to control, manipulate, or even rationalize the chaos. In fact, according to the legend, on St. Meinrad's first day as a hermit in the ominously dark forest, he rescued a pair of black ravens from a predator hawk. This is both illuminating and fascinating when you consider that in the story of Isis, the Sacred Black Feminine supergoddess of Egypt, the hawk is a symbol of the sun and the patriarchal values of logic and linear thinking. The raven, on the other hand, represents the darker, more chaotic, and less controllable aspects of consciousness. Gustafson asserts, "Meinrad could have left the ravens to the hawk. That he did not reflects his attitude toward the unknown, the dark mysterious aspect of life which can all too easily be displaced by the kind of scholastic training and cultural background available to Meinrad."[2] By rescuing the ravens from the hawk, St. Meinrad affirmed his commitment to protecting and nurturing his growing connection to the divine darkness, the crucial aspect of spirituality that his life in Zurich could not nurture. But St. Meinrad didn't just rescue the ravens that day. He also rescued himself. By leaving Zurich and the monastery, St. Meinrad rescued his own inner spiritual raven from the hawk of patriarchal religion. But he didn't accomplish this feat alone. Our Lady of the Ominously Dark Forest, a Black Madonna in the lineage of Isis, accompanied St. Meinrad as he cared for both the physical ravens and the spiritual raven within.

Like the hawk, patriarchal religion wants to devour our inner raven because then we will never encounter our spiritual birthright as cherished children of the ancient Sacred Black Feminine, the "dark-skinned Holy Woman who is unafraid of any dark."[3] As Jill Melick writes, "To become whole, body and soul, we need to depart from the safety of the childhood house of beliefs into the wilderness, into the cave, with only the psychic necessities. We rarely have the safety of leaving one house of beliefs when we can clearly see the new house ahead lighted and warm. More often, we need to leave the old without any promise of the new, need to spend time as forest dwellers, just surviving."[4] Our time in the darkness is essential for our liberation for it is there that we discover that our patriarchal needs for certainty and control are interfering with our union with the Divine. Kristen Harper, healer, poet, and author of *Darkness Divine*, adds, "In the darkness exists a time of letting go to relax in God's embrace."[5]

Because Black Madonna lives in the darkness, when we encounter disappointment and disillusionment in our lives, we can rest assured that no matter what we are going through, if we seek her in the darkness, we will find her. When we are facing debilitating pain and disillusionment, the Black Madonna of the Ominously Dark Forest reminds us that we can actually surrender rather than run from the darkness because she is in the darkness. Even more, she *is* the darkness. As Gustafson writes, "The forest was *her* in her primitive undifferentiated state: the *prima materia*, the beginning substance" of the world.[6] The dark forest helps us connect with her essence: the ancient Sacred Black Feminine that existed before the world and birthed the world. In the presence of Black Madonna, where there is darkness there is new life. In her finsterwald, we experience the truth that theologian Emmanuel Katongole has long proclaimed: hope and lament are twin sisters walking hand in hand.[7] In other words, lament and hope are two sides of the same coin. If lament is present, hope is too. In the midst of disappointment, suffering, pain, and darkness, we can trust that regeneration and the birthing of new worlds are also present and available to us. Because our spirituality of darkness is often malnourished, we typically don't even look for hope and new life in the midst of pain, lament, and disappointment. But hidden within every disappointment is a magical seed of hope. When we spend time with the

Black Madonna of the Ominously Dark Forest, she helps us uncover, plant, germinate, and birth the hidden hope that accompanies pain.

Additionally, when we seek Black Madonna in the midst of darkness, we encounter her in a deeper and more liberating way than we would if we only communed with her when things were going well. An alchemist, she takes our pain and disillusionment and uses them to help us connect with her in a deeper, more empowering, and liberating way. In her ominously dark forest, Black Madonna shows us that we grow in the dark and that our liberation journeys are nurtured by the darkness. The Black Madonna of Einsiedeln assures us that our time as forest dwellers will be both liberating and fiercely accompanied by her.

Over time, St. Meinrad's solo hermitage expanded as other monks in search of the divine darkness joined him in the finsterwald. Eventually a monastery was built to accommodate the growing number of monks. In the center of the monastery church, the monks built a small chapel to house the Black Madonna of the Ominously Dark Forest. Today, the "Lady Chapel" remains at the central entrance to the vast church. St. Meinrad's legacy and commitment to divine darkness is still apparent today. Though Einsiedeln Abbey is a major pilgrimage destination and welcomes about one million visitors per year, the Benedictine monks who live there today are cloistered. In other words, they live in a closed, hermitlike community, only interacting with the public while engaging in ministry and performing essential tasks. Their ongoing commitment to embracing the divine darkness is reflected in their daily practice of singing the ancient "Salve Regina" ("Hail Queen") hymn to Black Madonna and in the monastery's flag, which simply depicts two black ravens.

THE TRANSFORMATIVE FIRE IN THE DARKNESS

If St. Meinrad left Zurich in search of a robust experience of darkness and chaos, then he definitely got what he was looking for. Beyond the bandits, animal predators, harsh alpine winters, and general lawlessness of the finsterwald, the monastery he founded was terrorized by frequent and voracious fires. From St. Meinrad's time until 1577, a period of 716 years, the monastery was destroyed by five different fires—"a crude reminder of the capricious nature of life, of those unexpected unknowns in life that take as easily as they give."[8] Each time, the entire monastery was destroyed except for Black Madonna's Lady Chapel, which according to tradition always remained untouched by the fire. After each fire, the monastery buildings were rebuilt around the Lady Chapel. Conventional wisdom often sends people running *away* from the smoky flames when they discover that there is a fire in their midst. But over time, the monks and village people became convinced that the only safe refuge during a monastery fire was in the center of the monastery in the miraculous Lady Chapel with Black Madonna. Consequently, rather than running *away* from the fiery monastery, they ran *toward* its center because they knew that the only way to survive the fire was to stand by the inextinguishable Black Madonna. They knew that in her holy embrace, no fire could destroy them, and that all could be made new.

In Black Madonna's holy embrace, life's fires become a magical tool for transformation and renewal rather than destructive torment. Gustafson draws a helpful connection between the frequent monastery fires and the transformative fires of medieval alchemists. He writes, "Fire was often the *prima materia* from which a more refined product emerges. It was also a part of the *incineratio*, the burning and bringing to ashes before change can take place. The monastery fires did not just signify destruction, but also a means of renewal and further development. . . . In other words, [Black Madonna] represents that psychic force which not only sustains but also destroys and brings to life again."[9] Paradoxically, the Black Madonna of the Ominously Dark Forest doesn't promise that we will never face darkness or experience the capricious, unexpected, and painful aspects of life. But she does promise that when life's inevitable fires descend upon us, if we run *toward* her rather than *away* from her, she will embrace us, stand with us, and show us how to not only survive the fires but rise anew. She does this by using the fire to burn off the attachments, identities, and ideas that are no longer serving us so that we can rise from the ashes empowered and free to embrace our birthright identities as her holy children of the fire who do not fear the fire because we know that we have been formed by the fire. With her by our side, the fiery and antagonistic hellscapes of our lives become fertile with nourishing wisdom, protection, intimacy with the Divine, and hope.

The white patriarchal god is a boogeyman who sends every wild-fire of oppression and pain our way because he wants to scare us into believing that we are alone in the fire and can be destroyed by the fire. He's the god of the Heaven-and-Hell house of my youth who tries to spook us with his fiery hellscape and send us running back to the sanitized, predictable, and highly controlled "Heaven" because he knows that if we truly encounter the Divine in darkness, he will no longer be able to control us with his rigid, dehumanizing, racist, and sexist "law and order." He knows that if we follow Meinrad's footsteps into the magical finsterwald, we will be transformed into saints too. The white patriarchal god knows that if, like St. Meinrad, we learn to look for the Divine in the fiery and chaotic hellscape, the flames of oppression will no longer extinguish our hope, for we will know that God herself is with us in the fiery hellscape and carrying us as we navigate through it. He knows that if we discover that she is with us in the fiery hellscape, we will learn that his fire cannot devour her because she is the *prima materia* that birthed the world from fire. And he knows that if we commune with her for long enough in the fire, we will discover that we are cut from the same cloth as our prehistoric Sacred Black Feminine Mother, and that we too are the *prima materia*. When we burn, we are not devoured. Like our ancient Mother, when we burn, we birth new worlds.

BLACK MADONNA'S RADIANTLY DARK WOMB

As Our Lady of the Ominously Dark Forest, Black Madonna shows us that darkness is an invitation to surrender and commune deeper with the Divine in the midst of darkness. In order to survive the finster-wald, we must surrender our need to control and understand it and instead receive its wisdom. Similarly, in order to survive the darkness, we must surrender our need to control and understand it and instead receive Black Madonna's wisdom. Of course, this is easier said than done. Yet I believe the Black Madonna of the Ominously Dark Forest illuminates our path to surrender. I know she did it for me.

Even before I consciously began my journey toward Black Madonna, I'd been deeply uncomfortable with Christianity's "spirituality of darkness," in which, generally speaking, God is present in the light and absent in the darkness. Not only is it racist to associate light with good and darkness with evil, it is also reductive, unimaginative, and flimsy.[10] (No surprise here. "Reductive, unimaginative, and flimsy" are markers of white patriarchal thinking.) So even when I tried to reject "darkness = bad" thinking, I was left with little to guide my spiritual imagination beyond this point.

Okay, so God is not necessarily absent in the darkness. Now what? Now what do I do? How do I engage with the Divine when I encounter unyielding pain, disillusionment, uncertainty, and trepidation? And how do I engage with the Divine when, as a Black woman, it seems that my life is one long continuous string of disillusionment, uncertainty, and trepidation?

Per my modus operandi, I spent years trying to "reclaim darkness" by devouring great books like Mirabai Starr's jaw-dropping translation of St. John of the Cross's *Dark Night of the Soul* and by trying to make sense of vague spiritual-speak like "but the light is most apparent in the night!" In my early 30s, I even tried to communicate a different approach to darkness in a widely read Advent essay. But none of this quite set my spiritual imagination free, much less empowered it to build something new.

I also began to recognize that our impoverished spirituality of darkness is one of white patriarchy's ploys to keep us in its limiting fold—for it is directly into darkness's uncertainty that we must march if we are ever to liberate ourselves. As philosopher Bayo Akomolafe points out, our enslaved ancestors who dared to escape the plantation didn't immediately encounter the certainty and clarity of freedom. Rather, their escape led them into the uncertainty of fugitivity. Just as contending with uncertainty was a necessary step on our ancestors' freedom road, contending with uncertainty is a necessary step on our freedom road.[11] If we don't have any tools to unshackle our spiritual imaginations and guide our discovery, we will be forever confined to the plantation of what is, never able to become the liberation-bound forest dwellers who commune with Black Madonna in the finsterwald.

I needed to do more than simply reject the flimsy spirituality of darkness that I was taught. I needed a new way, a new metaphor, a new spiritual foundation from which to build. That's when I realized that I not only needed to reexamine my language for God but also reexamine my language about God. And I needed to reject the "house of beliefs" that just wasn't working for me so I could discover something new.

Thank Goddess, in early 2020 I was introduced to archaeologist Marija Gimbutas's vast body of illuminating work. Gimbutas, who was celebrated for her groundbreaking study of the earliest religions, described how the majority of the earliest images of the Sacred Black Feminine highlight the womb and/or umbilical cord. In her archaeological digs, she encountered numerous prehistoric statues and etchings that showed humans/lesser gods forever connected to the Sacred Black Feminine via the umbilical cord. Gimbutas's research suggests that early humans understood that the umbilical cord is more than an anatomical reality. It's also a spiritual reality, forever inviting humanity into radical dependence upon the Divine.

My reading of Gimbutas's books and articles coincided with the first COVID-19 shelter-in-place order in Oakland, where I was living at the time. During one of my regular walks through the redwood forest near my house, I noticed that the moist redwood forest canopy, which blocked out almost all the sunlight, felt very womb-like. And that's when it hit me. As I carried uncertainty around the global liminal space of COVID-19, as well as uncertainty around my own personal liminal spaces, it occurred to me that "womb" is a more life-giving metaphor than "darkness."

Though not all women have wombs and not all womb-holders are women, Black Madonna's female body offers us a powerful metaphor for how we are held, nourished, and supported in the midst of darkness. As Ursula K. Le Guin teaches us, "Women grow things in darkness, not in light."[12] Black Madonna's cosmic womb, the same womb that birthed our world many millions of years ago, offers us a liturgical promise that our time in the darkness is not in vain. Kristen Harper writes, "The dark womb pushed out the light that released the heavens and cradled the planets and stars adorning the universe; it formed the darkened earth from which all life emerged and to which all life returns when our bodies take their final breaths. It is the same darkness that shelters us from an unrelenting sun; that calls animals to safe hibernation; that protects the germination of seed and bulb."[13] Black Madonna's cosmic womb assures us that our time in the darkness *will* lead to restoration and growth.

Yet as a Black woman, I am painfully aware that the womb metaphor is a complicated one as the womb has been a site of chaos, pain, and disempowerment for many Black people. Throughout U.S. history, Black wombs have been hyperpoliced by the white patriarchal society, and Black people have been stripped of their womb sovereignty and power to make our own choices about our bodies, wombs, and fetuses. For example, during chattel slavery, when Black people were forcibly impregnated in order to increase the enslaved population, the Black womb was reduced to a baby-producing factory that existed solely to generate white wealth. Since then, Black people have been sterilized without our consent,[14] forced to bring fetuses to term without our consent, and have had our infants punitively abducted by Child Protective Services at birth.[15] During the months I worked on this chapter, Adriana Smith, a Black woman in Georgia who was nine-weeks pregnant when she experienced a brain trauma and was legally declared dead, was forced to remain on life support because the state's white patriarchal abortion laws required her to carry the fetus to term. Adriana languished for four months until she delivered an extremely preterm baby boy named Chance via emergency C-section—at which point she was promptly taken off life support.[16] This gut-wrenching story underscores the reality that Black people do not have autonomy over our wombs—in either life or death. Even more, little Chance, who was just 1 pound, 13 ounces at birth, has a hard road ahead of him, a rude reminder of how inhospitable this world is for Black bodies.

In addition to being hyperpoliced, the Black womb is also violently neglected in our white patriarchal society. Maternal mortality data recently released by the U.S. Centers for Disease Control and Prevention show that Black women are more than three times more likely to die during childbirth than white women and significantly more likely to die during childbirth than both Hispanic and Asian women. Additionally, due to advances in the field of obstetrics, maternal mortality has significantly decreased for white, Hispanic, and Asian women. However, maternal mortality has significantly increased for Black women, despite the advances in medicine.[17] These research findings reveal systemic anti-Blackness in the medical field, an industry that frustratingly develops techniques that support all wombs *except* Black wombs.

Due to these historical and current realities, the Black womb is a place of both life *and* death, both safety *and* peril, both nurturing *and* neglect, and both hope *and* lament. In other words, the Black womb is much like the finsterwald—a complex, unpredictable, and often unsafe place that simultaneously also holds the immense capacity to birth new life. This is all the more reason why Black Madonna's Black womb can be such a powerful metaphor for us—for only a cosmic Black womb can adequately speak to and hold our complex, certainty-stripping finsterwald experiences. Black Madonna, whose Black womb was also hyperpoliced in the birth story of the historical Jesus, intimately understands the pain that Black people experience as womb-holders and can expertly attend to this very specific finsterwald. At the same time, as the ancient Sacred Black Feminine, Black Madonna has seen everything and can relate to everyone. In truth, her womb is so dark precisely because, like the color black, it contains all the colors and experiences across human existence. There is no pain, chaos, disappointment, oppression, or fear that cannot be held, nurtured, and healed by her womb. Regardless of race, gender, or whether our pain is womb related or not, we can bring our finsterwald experiences to Black Madonna's womb that is so dark that it radiates.

Interestingly, one of the few existing pregnant Black Madonnas in the world underscores this point. The magnificent 11th-century Black Madonna of Mende, France, is traditionally called the Queen of the City and the County. She is a disarming and captivating Black Madonna, and when I visited her in 2018, I couldn't take my eyes off her. More than any other Black Madonna I have visited, she looks the most like a Buddha. Deep in meditation and with her eyes closed, she is serene and alone, accompanied only by the fetus inside her visibly pregnant body. Though she looks like she's in her third trimester, her body is a refuge of peace and rest. I love that the people who venerate her in Mende call her the Queen of the City and the County. Though she is at peace and she is at rest, she is not to be trifled with! She is *in charge*. She's the Queen of the City *and* County. There is no place where she doesn't reign. There's no place where she isn't protecting and guiding her loved ones, no place where she isn't offering comfort and care, no place where she isn't nourishing and healing. As the Queen of the City and the County, she can truly handle it all—and her Black and cosmic womb beckons all to find rest and refuge within.

The invitation to experience Black Madonna's Black and cosmic womb as a universal refuge of nurturing, guidance, and flourishing can be immensely liberating. Her Black and cosmic womb can hold what we cannot hold ourselves. When we surrender our finsterwalds to it, we get a chance to breathe a little bit more as we discover that her womb is fueling our growth, healing, and birth process while simultaneously soothing our uncertainty and pain.

Surrender is the key word here.

Imagine a fetus saying to the womb-holder, "Hey, I've been ruminating about life after birth and I'm stressed about what it will be like and how I will survive and whether you will reliably provide for me." It sounds preposterous because obviously a fetus doesn't have the cognitive ability to imagine the future, much less stress about it! And that is exactly why the fetus is able to relax into dependence and intimacy. Without an ability to rely on its own analysis of the situation, the fetus must rely on the parent, despite the uncertainty. The fetus must surrender to the womb; there is no other way to be free.

But our adult higher-order cognitive thinking gets us into trouble. Rather than surrendering to the womb as the fetus does, we ruminate on every possible threat, both real and imagined. Since we are accustomed to relying on (read: idolizing) the information we glean from our senses, we devolve into even greater panic when we encounter situations that we cannot sense or reason our way out of. My human instinct to devolve into greater panic amid liminal spaces is why a flimsy spirituality of darkness never worked for me. Liminal spaces are legitimately scary, and as a human I have built-in coping mechanisms that actually prevent me from connecting with the Divine when I need her most. But I'm beginning to imagine a spirituality of the womb that offers a pathway to connection in the midst of it all.

When I think of a liminal space as a womb space instead of a dark space, many more possibilities open. I can exhale deeply and begin to relinquish my need to make sense of everything and independently navigate my way. I can release the unknown and the unknowable to the trustworthy womb of Black Madonna. For as Gustafson asserts, "What the collective order cannot accept, the Black Madonna can."[18]

Black Madonna's Black and cosmic womb gives us a place to stop carrying the burden of the liminal space and instead be carried.

Black Madonna's Black and cosmic womb offers us a nurturing place to go when we are grappling with uncertainty.

Black Madonna's Black and cosmic womb assures me that we will experience new birth on the other side of this liminal space.

Black Madonna's Black and cosmic womb promises spiritual abundance, even when we don't know what's going to happen next.

Black Madonna's Black and cosmic womb declares that we are completely surrounded by love's life force no matter what is going on.

Black Madonna's Black and cosmic womb offers a profound invitation to rely more on the Divine Parent when we cannot sense or think our way out of uncertainty. In this way, we are invited into an even deeper dependence that begins to chip away at uncertainty. The fetus connected to the umbilical cord is faced with zero uncertainty. Its needs are fully addressed. Its pain is immediately attended to.

Black Madonna's Black and cosmic womb gives us a spiritual umbilical cord that activates precisely when we are faced with uncertainty. We can trust that if we reach for the cord, it will nourish us with the outlook, wisdom, and love that we need in that moment.

BLACK MADONNA'S SACRED UMBILICAL CORD BREATHES HEALING LIFE INTO OUR PAIN

I currently live in Minneapolis, Minnesota, the home of George Floyd. As I was writing this chapter, many Minneapolis citizens were commemorating the five-year anniversary of his brutal, state-sanctioned execution in 2020. Floyd's memory reverberates throughout the city in the homemade signs and graffiti that ominously echo his last cries: "I can't breathe, I can't breathe!"

One reason why George Floyd's murder resonates so deeply with many Black people is that many of us can relate to his desperate call for help in the face of society's savage dehumanization of Black people. As a Black woman, I have struggled to breathe my entire life. Yet I was well into my 30s before I began learning to notice when I couldn't breathe. For years I wasn't breathing, but I didn't know it.

As a child, my spiritual community taught me that Black women are responsible for everyone else's physical and emotional well-being. In order to meet everyone else's needs, and keep everyone else happy, I dissociated from myself, my body, my needs, my breath, my humanity, and my divinity. The more I ignored my own breath, the more I was applauded and affirmed by my community for being "good," "faithful," and "selfless."[19] My experience isn't unique. Speaking to Black women, storyteller Upile Chisala affirms: "You were taught to work miracles for everyone but yourself. A messiah to others but barely a friend of your own."[20] And Alice Walker adds, "Black women are called . . . 'the mule of the world,' because we have been handed the burdens that everyone else—everyone else—refused to carry. We have been called 'Matriarchs,' 'Superwomen,' and 'Mean and Evil Bitches.' . . . When we have pleaded for understanding, our character has been distorted, when we have asked for simple caring, we have been handed empty insipid appellations, then stuck in the furthest corner."

As a Black woman, Black Madonna intimately understands the very particular type of pain, disillusionment, and uncertainty that Black people face around the globe. It is precisely because she is Black that she is able to empathize with our cries. As a Black female deity that white patriarchal religion has repeatedly tried to suffocate and extinguish across the millennia, she echoes our cries. In the darkness of her womb, she holds, soothes, and restores the parts of us that have been harmed and erased by white patriarchy and its glaring sun. Harper vocalizes this powerful gospel: "Truth is, my heart is already broken and the sun sees it not. The blazing fire in the sky does not allow me to speak more easily, to name my suffering and bask in its flare. But in the dark, my tears can fall in relief. In the dark my scars fade and I can sense the healing. In the dark I find freedom and can finally be brave."[21] Within her womb and via her sacred umbilical cord, Black Madonna shows us how to move through our pain and disillusionment with her by our side.

Black Madonna intimately understands our cries of *I can't breathe*. Though society is often antagonistic or indifferent to the cries of Black people, when we surrender our struggling gasps to her, she lovingly and immediately sends her ancient Sacred Black Feminine breath to us through her sacred umbilical cord. In doing so, she transforms our cries of *I Can't Breathe* into a declaration of our humanity. Black Madonna, who is a target of white patriarchy precisely because she defends the most marginalized and speaks truth to power, is modeling for us how to be *human* in a world that sees us as *mules*. She's showing us how to notice our edges, our burdens, our pain, our limits, our breath, our bodies—and how to *name* and *proclaim* them. She's helping us follow in the footsteps of powerful and wise Black women like Harper, who declares, "Fierceness is breathing through, not denying the pain. It is claiming the scars, not covering them up. It is owning the anger, letting it flow out of parted lips, pointed fingers, a tilted head—not letting it possess or alter my spirit."[22] Regardless of how much society ignores our cries, we get to exert our right to be human, to breathe deeply, and to say "Not today, colonizer. *I am not your mule*." Though white patriarchy may try to punish us for affirming our humanity, Black Madonna stands beside us echoing our *no* and affirming our humanity.

Even more, by responding to our cries of "I can't breathe" with a deep gust of sacred breath, Black Madonna is modeling what it looks like to ground ourselves in our breath. She's teaching us that we can find power in our connection to her. In doing so, she's confirming that our cries of "I can't breathe" are also a declaration of our divinity. By helping us reconnect to our breath, to her, and to the earth, she's showing us how to move through pain and disillusionment without losing our sacred connection to ourselves, to her, and to the earth. In addition to being disconnected from our bodies, Black women have been disconnected from the earth. Slavery, domestic servitude, environmental racism, and the gross devaluing of Black women's labor have antagonized Black women's sacred relationship to the earth. She's reversing and healing the ways that white patriarchy has disconnected us from the earth, which is also her.

In honor of George Floyd, I recently embarked on a long contemplative walk. As I moved through my predominantly Black neighborhood, I began to verbally proclaim my sacred relationship to the earth. Relishing the luxurious spring sun and attuning to the orchestra of birds, I experienced what theologian and poet Lady Dane Figueroa Edidi calls "hearing the psalms of nature." As I connected to my breath and to the earth, I was acutely reminded that Black Madonna is right here, in my neighborhood, in the thick of it. She's in the breath, wind, sun, and soil. And because she is of the earth and we are of the earth, we are forever resourced. We only need to call out, "I can't breathe" so we can reconnect with the Divine in ourselves and in her.

As I surveyed the Black urban landscape, I thought of the long lineage of Black women who couldn't breathe, including my ancestors as well as younger versions of myself. Breathing in, I whispered, "I see you there, pain." Breathing out, I whispered, "I'm holding you gently in the dark." As I walked, Black Madonna whispered and breathed within me.

Even more than a declaration of our humanity and divinity, Black Madonna affirms that our cries of *I can't breathe* are a clarion call. In the midst of pain, disillusionment, and uncertainty, when we share our *I can't breathe* with her, she joins us in saying enough is enough! *I can't breathe* is the rallying cry of mother bears who refuse to acquiesce to the status quo, who refuse to back down from a fight. It's the hymn of the Black Madonna of Hal, who catches cannonballs with her bare hands while breastfeeding. *I can't breathe* is Black Madonna–speak for *aw hell naw*.

As a clarion call, *I can't breathe* means it's time to say *no* on a cosmic level; it means that #timesup. *I can't breathe* is fueled by righteous anger. It's a declaration that walls, both inner walls and outer walls, need to come down—and they need to come down *now*. When we vulnerably offer our *I can't breathe* to Black Madonna, she shows us that she's both love *and* love-in-action, and says, "C'mon, kids. We're busting out of this joint."

Finally, *I can't breathe* is a primal-celestial birthing force. If you've ever given birth or witnessed a birthing, you likely know that there is a deeply human but also otherworldly moment at which the birth parent has been pushing and screaming and writhing and breathing and crying for what seems like forever, and they literally cannot handle the process any longer. You can see it on their face, "Okay, *this* cannot go on any longer. This baby's coming out *now*." On the edge of exhaustion, the birth parent connects with their deepest, primal strength for one last big push. And at this point, there's literally nothing that can stop that baby from coming out.

I can't breathe is the last big push, our last gasp of surrender to Black Madonna's radiant darkness. When we offer her our *I can't breathe*, she knows we're ready. She knows that we know it's time to work miracles for ourselves.

Because Black Madonna intimately understands our cries of *I can't breathe*, her radiantly dark womb has a built-in mechanism to infuse us with her nourishing breath while also relieving us of our pain: the sacred umbilical cord. Though the human umbilical cord is one single cord, it has two main functions. One function is to take out the fetus's waste products. The other function is to provide the fetus's oxygen supply and the nutrients needed to grow and thrive. In the outgoing direction, the umbilical cord takes out the trash, so to speak. And in the incoming direction, it breathes life and nourishment into the fetus.

We too can release our painful "trash" to Black Madonna and trust that life and nourishment will be returned to us. Like the umbilical cord, the breath is bidirectional, with both outgoing and incoming processes. Like clockwork, the exhale releases and the inhale receives. With each *I can't breathe* we offer to her, we release the pain, uncertainty, disappointment, and disillusionment to the outgoing flow of the umbilical cord. And in response to our release, she returns life and nourishment to us.

SURRENDERING TO HER RADIANTLY DARK WOMB

These days, I am full of pain and disillusionment. I thought I'd find community and kinship in the world of Black Madonna devotees—but by and large, I haven't.

As a refugee from white evangelicalism—a spiritual community that is theologically incapable of honoring the sacredness of my Black female embodied soul—my whole being longed for acceptance and belonging in the divine feminine spiritual world. Tragically, it didn't take long for me to discover that the problem of anti-Blackness is just as prevalent among "woke" and "feminist" goddess devotees as it is in white evangelicalism. Much to my anguish, I realized that in the divine feminine world my cries of *I can't breathe!* continued erupting as I encountered prominent teachers and communities that relentlessly centered their white, elitist perspectives, erased Black and brown women's embodied experiences, and relegated my beloved Black Madonna to a subservient mammy-god who exists solely to make white women feel comfortable.

Not too long ago, I was seething over a gaggle of divine feminine teachers—all white women—who were acting violent, like typical white feminists. After a frustrating and painful online encounter with these women, my whole body puffed up with (self-)righteous anger. My eyes glared. My neck stood tense and erect. My veins revealed themselves. My breath escalated into booming huffs and puffs.

"*I can't breathe,*" I roared as my gut hardened and expanded, as if I had just gorged on Chipotle for lunch and now had to contend with an overgrown food baby.

These women were wrong, wrong, wrong and I had the rage baby to prove it.

I've learned enough about myself to know that holding on to this suffocated rage baby would not be a life-giving or sustainable option. I knew this rage baby would birth nothing but more rage and an autoimmune disease flare-up. So I did what my wild and fierce teacher Andrew Harvey instructed me to do during the first class I ever took on the divine feminine: When I'm raging at injustice, I need to stop fixating on the wrong and simply dance and breathe it out with Black Madonna. "As you move, she'll soothe your heart and your lungs and reveal your next steps to you," Andrew told our class years and years ago.

Though it was counterintuitive at first, I've been following Andrew's wise guidance for years now, so much so that the sacred impulse to dance and breathe it out with Black Madonna is almost as instinctive as my impulse to rage. I'm not a table person, so I always turn the dining area in my home into a dance-breathe-dream space that's ever ready for my regular dance-a-thons with Black Madonna.

So dance and breathe I did. And as I moved with fury, I told Black Madonna all about her horrible white daughters (as if the All-Wise One needed me to brief her on them).

I stomped my feet, huffed and puffed, and raged, "They're out here disrespecting your Black body."

I shook my booty and roared, "These white women claim to love you but don't want to talk about their white supremacy."

I wagged my fingers and hollered, "They call themselves daughters of the Dark Mother. Hmph. More like Daughters of the Confederacy."

I shook and twerked and quaked until I was out of breath and words.

As my swaying hips slowed, I heard Black Madonna gently whisper over my left shoulder, "Precious Christena, those women don't own me."

"Damn right they don't own you," I smugly affirmed, expecting her to appreciate my two cents.

"And neither do you!" she retorted.

My swinging hips came to an immediate halt.

Yikes. Her words echoed throughout my motionless body, ricocheting like pinballs in an arcade game. Humbled, I yielded.

"And neither do I," I whispered to Black Madonna in the stillness.

In that moment of embodied truth, my entire nervous system relaxed and the wisdom that my rage had suppressed rose to the surface. I began to see that in response to my pain, I was trying to play God rather than exalt God. Like white patriarchy, I was trying to control the narrative about Black Madonna rather than allowing her to speak directly to her children and control her own narrative. Like white patriarchy, I was so caught up in my haughtiness that I thought it was more important to correct people than to go get humbly grounded in Black Madonna's love so that if I spoke up at all, it was by her heeding, according to her wishes, and absolutely devoid of self-righteousness.

When I surrender to Black Madonna, I can let go of my need to control myself, others, or the outcome of my experience of darkness. In essence, when God is a Black woman, I don't have to play God.

All that wisdom, guidance, and release was revealed in one frenetic breathe-and-dance session with Black Madonna's radiantly dark womb.

When we bring our fiery pain to Black Madonna, she receives it with empathy and care and transforms it into a deeper union with her. She shows us that the fire cannot consume us if we stand with her and allow her to alchemize the fire into liberating wisdom. When we seek her in the finsterwald, she meets us in the depths of our darkness and abides with us, forever reminding us that we are never alone in the dark. When we release our pain to her sacred umbilical cord, she rewards us with everlasting breath and the exact guidance we need to move through the pain and relax in her loving arms. The magical antidote to our impoverished spiritual imaginations, Our Lady of the Finsterwald forever exists in the Swiss alpine finsterwald so we'll never forget that God herself is with us in the darkness, in the heart of midwinter, in the fallow seasons, in the pain, in the *I can't breathes*, and in the fire.

There is no pain that she cannot transform, no expired breath that she cannot resuscitate, no death that cannot be reborn. For she herself is the radiant darkness—and in her darkness, everything grows.

SACRED UMBILICAL CORD
BREATHING CHORUS

Beloved, Black Madonna wants to dance and breathe with you in her radiantly dark womb. Unlike the white patriarchal god who is shackled to the mind and aimlessly wanders the halls of the ivory tower, Black Madonna is all about embodied wisdom and strategic street smarts. She speaks to us through our individual and collective bodies, meets us at our pain and gives us exactly what we need, and guides our next steps toward ushering her healing into the world. She doesn't require fancy degrees, TED Talks, or podcasts. She just wants to dance and breathe and reveal herself as a trustworthy womb-holder whose sacred umbilical cord will never fail you.

In their Black Feminist Breathing Chorus, Alexis Pauline Gumbs and Sangodare offer a wonderful practice for using the breath and repetition to nurture deeper communion with ancient wisdom. In the practice, a simple mantra is repeatedly and gently chanted 108 times (or for approximately 14 minutes) along with the natural rhythm of the breath. The repetition allows the wisdom of the mantra to sink more deeply into our embodied psyches so that it becomes as natural as the rhythm of the breath. I've loved chanting the power 21 mantras that Gumbs and Sangodare have gleaned from the lives of 21 Black feminist visionaries.

I've also noticed that the structure of this practice is well suited for an inhale/exhale sacred umbilical practice, so when I am lost in a finsterwald, when the fires of life are threatening to consume me, when I can't breathe, or when I can't make sense of my senseless pain—I surrender to Black Madonna's radiantly dark womb by adapting the Black Feminist Breathing Chorus format. I set my alarm for 14 minutes, turn on a soothing playlist, allow my body to relax, and then begin repeatedly breathing and chanting:

- With the exhale: "I see you there, pain."

- With the inhale: "I'm holding you gently in the dark" or "She's holding me gently in the dark."

I invite you to try this practice for yourself, especially when you are filled with pain and disillusionment and desperately need Black Madonna to abide with you in the dark. Feel free to use the chant that I created or write your own chant that invites her sacred umbilical cord to receive your pain and return wisdom and power to you.

I invite you to notice:

- Your physical sensations and emotions before, during, and after the practice. Did anything shift? Deepen? Stay the same? Go numb? Spike?

- Whether this practice helps you surrender to her radiantly dark womb. If so, how do you know?

7
INVOCATION

Black Madonna, our most faithful Co-Conspirator,
We raise our voice in gratitude.
When the plantation conditioned us to be small,
To live diminished, live in fear,
You appeared to us and thundered,
"You're too sacred for this"
As you marched us into freedom.
Black Madonna, our most faithful Co-Conspirator,
We clothe ourselves in adoration.

Black Madonna, our most faithful Source,
We raise our voice in gratitude.
First birther, ever birthing—
You are our first dawn, our first matriarch,
First mother, first night.
Each time patriarchy tries to extinguish your life force,
Indomitably, you rise, reborn—
Same essence, different form,
As you show us we too can be reborn.
Black Madonna, our most faithful Source,
We clothe ourselves in adoration.

Black Madonna, our most faithful Huntress,
We raise our voice in gratitude.
When the powers of this world alienated us from you,
When they lied and told us that God is white
And male and distant and cruel,
You crossed oceans and transfigured,

To abide, protect, and lavish us
With your never-ending love.
Black Madonna, our most faithful Huntress,
We clothe ourselves in adoration.

Black Madonna, our most faithful Guide,
We raise our voice in gratitude.
When life feels like a booby-trapped maze
And our burdens grind down on our souls,
You pluck us with your powerful hands and
Plant us on your life-giving labyrinth
As you remind us that you hold it all
so we don't have to.
Black Madonna, our most faithful Guide,
We clothe ourselves in adoration.

Black Madonna, our most faithful Defender,
We raise our voices in gratitude.
When fiery cannonballs surrounded,
And we were hopeless, convinced we were abandoned,
You emerged from the ashes and chaos,
Our great shield, your spectacular power you revealed.
Simultaneous defender and nurturer,
As your cosmic breast milk nourished us,
You held us close and soothed and sang
That as your sacred children we can catch cannonballs too.
Black Madonna, our most faithful Defender,

We clothe ourselves in adoration.
Black Madonna, our most faithful Darkness,
We raise our voices in gratitude.
Your radiant darkness burst open the lie
That you are confined to certainty, ease, and light.
Relieved, we followed you into your ominous forest,
Where you lovingly carried our pain and disillusionment
And placed them as sacraments on your holy transforming fire.
In your fecund darkness, we discovered the wonderful truth
That everything we need can be found in you.
Black Madonna, our most faithful Darkness,
We clothe ourselves in adoration.

Chapter 7

SHE FORTIFIES OUR HOPE

Cloaking Ourselves in Black Madonna's Miraculous Armor of Adoration

I know a woman who holds a senior leadership position in the Catholic academic community. She also happens to be an intersectional feminist who earnestly and tirelessly advocates for women's and LGBTQIA ordination, pro-choice policies, and progressive theologies within the larger Catholic Church. Honestly, her life sounds exhausting! So I once asked her how she continues to live and work within a white cis-heteropatriarchal community that doesn't support her liberatory efforts and often literally works to thwart them.

Her response? "Meh, the bishops will die."

My first thought was *How morbid!* My second thought was *Wait, are you in the Mafia? Are you planning a "hit" on the bishops?*

But then I realized that my friend's sentiment was simply a contemporary version of Harriet Tubman's 19th-century prophetic declaration, "My people are free! My people are free!" despite the very stark reality that millions of African-descended people were still enslaved at the time. About this declaration, historian Alexis Pauline Gumbs writes, "'My people are free!' was a bold statement for Harriet Tubman to make in the midst of U.S. chattel slavery, when the Fugitive Slave Act was in full effect and she herself was the most wanted fugitive slave in the land. However it was exactly that visionary certainty that guided Harriet Tubman to lead hundreds of enslaved people across constructed borders and to lead the largest successful uprising of enslaved people at the Combahee River."[1]

Though physical reality hopelessly insisted upon continued enslavement, Harriet was able to access a cosmic hope: that somehow, some way, reality would come into alignment with her people's freedom. Harriet knew that the U.S. laws, though clamorous and brutal, did not possess the cosmic authority to have the final say. Similarly, by saying, "Meh, the bishops will die," my friend meant that the bishops' influence is finite and that in the end, love and freedom will prevail. Like Harriet, she reliably experiences a cosmic hope even when life feels utterly hopeless. When she is rooted in this hope, she is not distracted by what the bishops are doing and not doing. When she abides with this hope, the bishops do not live rent free in her head because hope protects her from obsessing over the finite power of the bishops and relinquishing her power to them. Instead, her hope enables her to tap into the infinite vastness of the Divine so that her efforts are powered by a cosmic source. Her hope empowers her to continue her crucial efforts toward restoration, no matter the physical reality.

Throughout history, Black Madonna devotees have embodied a similar hope. Even when life is unbearably painful and dreary, people who love Black Madonna have known that they can rely on her to fortify their hope, redirect their focus, and direct them toward individual and collective freedom. In fact, the most famous prayer to Black Madonna is Memorare, which means "Remember" in Latin. The brief but potent 15th-century prayer begins with these lines:

> *Remember, O most gracious Virgin Mary,*
>
> *that never was it known that anyone who fled to your protection,*
>
> *implored your help, or sought your intercession,*
>
> *was left unaided.*
>
> *Inspired by this confidence,*
>
> *I fly unto you . . .*[2]

At first glance, it seems like the prayer is designed to jog Black Madonna's memory, to help her remember that she is, in fact, reliable. But in actuality, the first line is what Catholic scholars call an "Act of

Adoration." Such prayers are designed to remind the body of what the spirit already knows to be true: The Divine is present and powerful. In other words, the opening to the prayer is actually designed to jog *our* memories, not Black Madonna's memory. When we are in the throes of hopelessness, *we* need to be reminded that Black Madonna is present and powerful. Adoration brings our spirit and body together by helping our body remember the spiritual truth that Black Madonna is both present and powerful. In fact, research shows that prayers of adoration, such as the Memorare prayer, help the body relax.[3]

GETTING LOST IN THE VASTNESS OF BLACK MADONNA

I love the title "Megadonna." Though all 450-plus Black Madonnas are rightfully renowned for their unique, miracle-working powers, a handful of Black Madonnas are especially revered because they are exceptionally powerful. I call these superstars—such as the Black Madonna of Montserrat (Spain), the Black Madonna of Rocamadour (France), and the Black Madonna of Montevergine (Italy)—Megadonnas. Across the centuries Megadonnas have continually provided for, protected, healed, and transformed the tens of millions of people who have called out to them. Not just locally loved and worshipped, the world-famous Megadonnas attract devotees from across the globe and welcome millions of pilgrims each year.

A visit to the sanctuary of a Megadonna is the experience of a lifetime. Though the physical building may not be opulent or grandiose, the interior dazzles with thousands of ex-votos: tokens of gratitude from adoring pilgrims such as homemade paintings depicting a miracle, model ships offered in gratitude for a safe return from war, plaster or wax reproductions of body parts symbolizing healed ailments, and little metal charms inscribed with heartfelt sentiments. Though every Black Madonna sanctuary I've ever visited has been full of ex-votos, the number of ex-votos at a Megadonna sanctuary is staggering; the mere sight of them sends a lightning bolt of abundance through my body. Not surprisingly, Megadonnas receive so many ex-votos that their sanctuary caretakers must regularly clear them out in order to maintain the space and make room for the constant influx of new ones. Since Black Madonna is a fountain of abundance who perpetually offers her healing and powerful love, the miracles never stop, and the throngs of pilgrims offering ex-votos never subside. This is especially true for Megadonnas, whose sanctuaries filled with ex-votos often resemble a whimsical emporium of curiosities.

I can spend hours examining ex-votos—an apothecary jar filled with hair from a miracle baby's first haircut, a pocket-sized vintage candy tin full of seeds harvested after Black Madonna ended a drought, a crude clay bust of Black Madonna that would be mocked by art critics but oozes contagious hope, a commissioned painting about that one time the local volcano erupted in August and Black Madonna conjured a magical midsummer blizzard that halted the fiery lava and saved the village from destruction. Each ex-voto tells an intimate story about that particular Megadonna's miraculous intervention in regular people's lives. These are not the jaw-dropping stories involving kings and empires that are mentioned in the history books. Rather, they show a different aspect of Black Madonna's power, the part of her that is just as attentive to a peasant in physical pain as she is to a queen trying to save her people from an encroaching army.

The ex-votos shine a light on Black Madonna's heart of abundance and explain why devotees travel from far and wide to offer prayers of desperation and gratitude to Megadonna, who doesn't just care for her local constituents or for "important" global matters but roams the cosmos attending to the heartfelt prayers of all her people. Despite her power and fame, the people know that Megadonna hears the prayers of all her children and reliably intervenes in the everyday lives of everyday people: restoring a broken heart, answering a person's prayer for a lover, healing a broken limb, providing rain in the midst of drought, protecting a farmer's crop from a worm infestation, and other gifts of grace. The ex-votos are proof that Megadonnas are never too busy or too famous to shower their people with lavish, personalized care. The ex-votos are proof that at her core, Black Madonna wants to make everything in your life bloom.

In Megadonnas who possess massive power yet share it freely, we see that Black Madonna is the Mother of Abundance. Unlike the white patriarchal gods, Black Madonna doesn't hoard her power, reserve it for the upper class, or weaponize it to control people. Rather, she uses her power to shower abundance on all who seek it. She uses it to plant, restore, and nurture life within us. As the Mother of Abundance, Megadonna is always birthing abundance in us and around us, even in the midst of death.

In awe of these superstar Black Madonnas who balance astonishing power and fame with intimate care for their people, I began seeking a special name for them. I was thrilled when I encountered the work of multidisciplinary artist Damon Davis, from whom I borrowed the title Megadonna. In his 2018 exhibition *Darker Gods in the Garden of Low Hanging Heavens*, Davis created an immersive world governed by 12 gods, all Black. At the center of the world stands Megadonna, a fiercely beautiful, dark-skinned Black woman with piercing eyes made of diamonds and clenched teeth made of gold. Davis's Megadonna is equal parts alluring and fierce. Her diamond eyes sparkle while also piercing and probing the world that she governs. Her clenched gold teeth illuminate the way while also reminding you not to underestimate her protective power. When I first laid eyes on Davis's Megadonna, I was both drawn toward her and acutely aware that she embodies a power that is beyond my human comprehension.

According to Davis, Megadonna is "the mother and creator of all the Gods in the universe."[4] In Davis's immersive world, Megadonna created herself from nothing, then created the gods and planets around her. She is infinitely generative, always blooming, always creating, always ushering forth life. In other words, Davis's Megadonna is a modern-day image of our beloved Sacred Black Feminine, the world's first sacred archetype—and a wonderful title for our superstar Black Madonnas. It's also an incredible reminder of Black Madonna's infinite power and bottomless and indomitable love. Though Megadonnas spectacularly display the vast and powerful reliability of Black Madonna, we often fail to truly grasp it and allow it to fortify our hope. Despite our growing knowledge of Black Madonna's miracles, most of us embody a miracle-less spirituality that is typically devoid of true hope.

THE PRIVILEGE OF HOPELESSNESS

During my visit to Palestine, a group of activists generously hosted me at their community center in Balata Refugee Camp, the oldest and largest Palestinian refugee camp in the West Bank. The tiny camp and flimsy structures within were hastily constructed by the Israeli colonial settler government in 1950 as temporary housing for the 5,000 Palestinians whose homes and land Israeli settlers had literally just stolen. Since then the camp has essentially become permanent and has ballooned to more than 32,000 displaced Palestinians. Not surprisingly, residents of Balata face ongoing issues due to severe overcrowding, an onslaught of terrorizing raids by the Israel Defense Forces, malnutrition, high unemployment, insufficient infrastructure, and more.[5] And yet, as I spent time with the Palestinian activists, they embodied a profound hope that seemed to tap into a deeper well. When I asked one activist, Hanan, how he remained hopeful amid such a tragic and oppressive situation, he matter-of-factly responded, "Despair is a luxury of the bourgeoisie."

Year later, I still think about Hanan's response almost every day as I battle to maintain hope while facing blatant fascism and the destruction of any semblance of American democracy, continuing police brutality toward Black people, increased hatred for our Muslim brothers and sisters, the applauding of wildly oppressive legislation from wildly oppressive legislators, the continuing genocide in Gaza, the ongoing climate crisis, and more. I have also begun to think more deeply about why it is so hard for me, a privileged North American, to contend for hope in the midst of our harrowing global reality. It would seem that North Americans, with all of the relative privileges and freedom we still enjoy, would be at the top of the hope ladder—just doling hope out to the people below us who don't have access to resources that can improve their lives or lack the social height to see the big picture from atop the ladder. But I have found that in my own life (and in the lives of countless other Western activists), it's far too easy to slink into hopelessness, and ultimately disengagement, as I face the seemingly insurmountable obstacles to true healing and restoration. Hopelessness, it seems, is an artifact of privilege.

My Rwandan friends who live, worship, and make peace in Kigali regularly tell me that we Westerners are the impoverished ones. "We pray for you all. When you have so many material things, you can't really know what it means to truly turn to divine resources for all that you need: the power to forgive, food to feed your children, healing from the trauma of genocide, stability in the midst of an unstable society, hope to keep fighting HIV."

My friends are right. My Western privilege—my access to power, influence, and agency due to my social location—clogs the pipeline between me and Black Madonna, reducing my ability to receive the always present, always powerful flow of hope, comfort, and empowerment that she continuously offers. When faced with the tragedy of injustice, I have the option of turning toward other things that will bring me temporary solace: Netflix binges effectively numb my pain, and even a victory (of the bargain variety) at Nordstrom Rack goes a surprisingly long way toward boosting my (false) sense of power.

Even when Westerners labor for healing and restoration, we often engage in strategies that deplete us of hope. Millennia ago, a Hebrew psalmist described a dynamic that still resonates today when, referring to the people who held relative power, he wrote, "Some trust in political power, some in military might." This is in contrast to the oppressed people with whom he identified when he said, "[B]ut we trust in the Name of YHWH, our God!" (Psalm 20:7).

North Americans often put our faith in the weapons of empire: the strong critical thinking skills we acquired at our liberal arts college; the professional networks of attorneys, business leaders, clergy, and community leaders that we have on our speed dial; and the relative ease with which we can raise money for a good cause. These efforts might be fueled by good intentions, but they often lead us to focus on the finite weapons of colonialism rather than the infinite well of hope that is found only in the Divine. They lure our eyes, hearts, and busy bodies toward the finite issues of our world rather than the infinite power, wisdom, hope, and freedom that we can encounter if we simply stop and turn our eyes, hearts, and bodies toward Black Madonna's cosmic resources.

Ironically, it is often the people who are least impacted by systemic oppression who are the most paralyzed by hopelessness. Oftentimes, the Westerner's distance from global oppression leads to what social psychologists call "a collapse of compassion." When we encounter a tragedy that involves lots of people (as is often the case in global oppression), we are motivated to regulate our emotions, distancing ourselves from the immense pain that we would experience if we paid close attention to each individual story within the tragedy.

Joseph Stalin reputedly said, "One death is a tragedy; one million is a statistic." When we witness oppression in an up-close-and-personal way—such as if we're personally oppressed or in close relationship with a person who is oppressed—we tend to open the floodgates of compassion toward the one or few individuals with whom we have a personal connection. But when we witness oppression from a distance and this oppression affects masses of people (e.g., the oppression of the Palestinians), we are easily overwhelmed by the sheer numbers. Rather than fortifying our compassion in response to such need, it collapses our compassion and we disengage into hopelessness. After conducting research on this collapse of compassion, social psychologists Daryl Cameron and Keith Payne concluded that "large-scale tragedies in which the most victims are in need of help will ironically be the least likely to motivate helping."[6]

But when we are intimately connected to systemic pain and tragedy, either personally or through close relationships, we are often able to respond with compassion and hope. When visiting the New England Holocaust Memorial in Boston, I read the following inscription by a survivor named Geerda Weissman Klein: "Ilse, a childhood friend of mine, once found a raspberry in the camp and carried it in her pocket all day to present it to me that night on a leaf. Imagine a world in which your entire possession is one raspberry and you give it to your friend." Imagine a world in which the bearer of hope is a little girl who is so systematically oppressed that she has no logical reason to believe that she will even live to the end of the day. Nevertheless, she defiantly cares for her one treasure because she is hopeful that she will be able to give it to her friend at the end of the day.

Preacher and scholar Rev. Dr. Jeremiah Wright described a similar hope in a 1990 sermon: "With her clothes in rags, her body scarred and bruised and bleeding, her harp all but destroyed and with only one string left, she had the audacity to make music and praise God. . . . To take the one string you have left and to have the audacity to hope."[7]

Today most North Americans, including many Black people, have grown accustomed to living miracle-less spiritual lives. Compared to the majority of the world, we have everything we "need," so we never have to actually rely on divine resources for a miracle. But as we learn to respond to oppression with hope in Black Madonna, we can rely on the wisdom of Black Madonna devotees across time, who implicitly understood that adoration is the gateway to hope and miracle-seeking.

ADORATION AS THE GATEWAY TO MIRACLE-SEEKING

As I have scoured the medieval and ancient stories about Black Madonna and the people who have loved her, I've noticed a curious pattern that has invited me to rethink everything I thought I knew about Black Madonna pilgrimages. Though many devotees embarked on resource-consuming, death-defying pilgrimages out of desperate need (e.g., an incurable disease, a quickly advancing enemy army, or systemic oppression), in the process of conducting my research, I've discovered that almost half of the pilgrimages were actually adoration pilgrimages. In other words, people experienced something abundant in their lives (e.g., a miraculous healing, rain at the end of a drought, or protection from a plague) and attributed the abundance to Black Madonna. So out of mere gratitude, they traveled hundreds of miles across perilous terrain and at great expense to offer adoration and ex-votos at the altar of Black Madonna.

When I first encountered this pattern, I was both floored and chastened. I was floored because, though I've cultivated a gratitude practice over the years, I've never considered taking a costly pilgrimage simply to say thank you. My daily practice of jotting down three gratitudes has been consistent, but it's been fairly minimal and not particularly embodied. Further, I was chastened because I realized that so much of my embodied connection to Black Madonna is based on my need. That's not necessarily a bad thing; it's a human thing. Many people first seek out Black Madonna because they are in dire straits. My initial 400-mile walking pilgrimage in 2018 was primarily fueled by my grief and desperation. I can't even count the number of times I've dramatically flung myself at the feet of a Black Madonna shrine. But I'm beginning to recognize that adoration pilgrimages are just as central to the legacy of Black Madonna as desperation pilgrimages are. For example, in late 2022 when I visited what is likely the oldest Black Madonna statue in France in the small Provençal town of Manosque, I noticed that ex-voto plaques of adoration (*reconnaissance* in French, which means "recognition" or "gratitude") surrounded her altar. The abundance of ex-votos at Black Madonna shrines teaches us that the rituals that arise out of embodied adoration are just as important as the rituals that arise out of embodied desperation. But as I've returned to the spirituality of my roots, I've discovered that my Black American ancestors knew this truth too. Like Black Madonna devotees around the globe, Black Americans have a long and powerful spiritual tradition of adoration.

ADORATION IS A CORNERSTONE OF BLACK AMERICAN SPIRITUALITY

God is good all the time; all the time God is good.

This is the refrain I most closely associate with my grandmommy, a sweet and powerful woman who embodied the Black Pentecostal Holiness tradition of my origins more than anyone I know. No matter what disappointment she faced, no matter what oppressive force she encountered, she prophetically and emphatically insisted on God's ever-present goodness and provision. As a young girl with nascent cognitive abilities, I took Grandmommy's simple act of adoration at face value in the same way that I took rainbows at face value. I was unaware of the multiple layers, processes, and shades that gave breadth and depth to what appeared on the surface.

In my youth, I didn't make the connection between Grandmommy's fierce practice of adoration and her equally fierce resilience.

Rather, I thought that adoration was spiritual bypassing—a cheap form of transcendence that distracted from the *real* work of healing and equity. But as I grew into young adulthood and experienced our society's ferocious anti-Blackness, I began to see how white patriarchy is at work in every space, especially Christian churches and institutions. I was shocked and grieved, and my commitment to proclaiming God's goodness crumbled.

Thankfully, I encountered the wonderful writings of 20th-century civil rights leader, mystic, and theologian Howard Thurman, which showed me that Grandmommy's persistent adoration drew from a rich tradition of adoration in Black American spirituality, one that dates back to the enslaved people who, while facing unconscionable oppression, proclaimed in a Negro spiritual:

> *He's the King of Kings, and the Lord of Lords,*
> *Jesus Christ, the first and last,*
> *No man works like him.*
> *He built a platform in the air,*
> *No man works like him.*

In Thurman's books *Deep River* and *The Negro Spiritual Speaks of Life and Death*, I learned that our enslaved ancestors, like many other oppressed peoples in global history, had developed a sophisticated practice of adoration that encompassed both transcendence and immanence.[8] As the Negro spiritual continues:

> *He meets the saints from everywhere,*
> *No man works like him.*
> *He pitched a tent on Canaan's ground.*
> *No man works like him.*
> *And broke the Roman Kingdom down,*
> *No man works like him.*

It is clear that my enslaved ancestors' adoration did not just focus on a God in the sky who is distant from the plight of the oppressed. Rather, it also focused on God's flesh-and-blood, earthly action against the forces of colonialism. As they reminded themselves of

God's transcendent power throughout history, they also reminded themselves of God's immanent concern for oppressed people and ability to set them free. This remembering of both God's all-inspiring power and God's proven track record of working miracles enabled many of our Black ancestors to radically reject the white jesus of the plantation and keep hope alive amid the brutality of chattel slavery. Their rituals of adoration fueled their hope.

When I asked Dr. Gayraud Wilmore, who is widely considered to be the father of Black liberation theology, what it was like to pioneer a new and liberative way of thinking about Blackness and the Divine, he replied, "Young lady, I'm not the father of Black liberation theology. The mothers and fathers of Black liberation theology are the enslaved people who, under the scorching sun and at the sound of the cracking whip, looked up at the sky and declared, 'There is a Balm in Gilead. This I know. This I know.'"

By quoting a line from a Negro spiritual, Dr. Wilmore was showing me that our Black ancestors' hope, not his pioneering theological brilliance, planted the true seeds of Black liberation theology. Despite the legal and social reality of the Antebellum South, our ancestors prioritized adoration and were able to tap into a deeper reality that healing is attainable, Black dignity is possible, and hope is worth clinging to. They embodied this hope in a myriad of ways, including plantation escapes, slave rebellions, secret spiritual gatherings, Black love, commitment to community flourishing, and practices of self-care and self-affirmation that defied colonial programming.

ADORATION AS AN ALCHEMICAL GATEWAY

Like Black Madonna devotees across time, our Black ancestors understood the importance of adoration rituals. Over the last few years, I have followed in their footsteps and begun a daily adoration ritual. In my ritual, I identify a specific gratitude and then expound on it as concretely, illustriously, and loquaciously as I can. I also take time to declare truths about who Black Madonna is: compassionate, the Queen of Peace, a mother bear who fiercely protects her cubs, a Lover who knows our worst pain, the Source without source, the Enclosure of the God Whom Nothing Can Contain, and more. Most days I also do a little dance in adoration to Black Madonna on behalf of my gratitude. By dramatically, extensively, and physically expressing my gratitude, I bring my body into alignment with my heart.

One day, in the midst of this ritual of embodied adoration, a magical thing happened. I began to feel so much more grounded in hope and at home in my body. Even before anything in my personal life or the world had changed, I began to fall asleep with less anxiety, and I felt more quiet assurance that I was not alone and more empowered to be generous in my relationships and activism—trusting that everything I needed would be available when I needed it.

I realized that the ritual of embodied adoration, much like the ancient Memorare prayer, is spiritual composting. It allows us to sift through the entirety of our lives, intentionally search for the life-giving organic matter, and throw it back into the spiritual garden. When we seek out and savor the abundance—even the smallest scraps of it that we perhaps wouldn't otherwise notice, much less savor—it nourishes the soil that sprouts hope and weeds out the voices that threaten to choke our hope.

It's easy to meditate on how racist or sexist or ignorant or entitled the oppressor is. But while those meditations are often true, they aren't particularly fortifying. Speaking the truth about Black Madonna's awe-inspiring power, genuine care for our lives, and proven track record of working miracles fortifies us by expanding our hearts and enabling us to receive the boundless hope of Black Madonna, even during moments of distress. As Andrew Harvey writes, "Constant adoration is the one force nuclear enough in its intensity to do this great work. Constant adoration, constant opening of the heart, in whatever circumstance, in whatever pain, in whatever difficulty and whatever grief, in whatever bitterness. Constant opening in adoration to divine beauty, the divine magnificence, the divine generosity, of all the different names of God. . ."[9] Similarly, artist and scholar Justin Randolph Thompson makes a helpful distinction between *ingesting* the wisdom of Black Madonna and *digesting* the wisdom of Black Madonna. It's easy to ingest knowledge about Black Madonna and claim devotion to her. But adoration helps us digest what we are learning and be wholly transformed by her. Adoration cements our devotion and makes us true devotees who are ready to courageously follow her leadership, no matter where it takes us.[10]

Though I once mistakenly believed that adoration was escapism, I now experience it as fortification. It is through the practice of adoration that we are armed with the strength to skillfully and fiercely face what is broken, incomplete, or seemingly hopeless. Through the practice of adoration, we are humbled and liberated by the reality that we do not fight alone—that Black Madonna, the Slave Mama of the oppressed, is *with* us and *for* us. When we clothe ourselves in adoration, our hope is fortified and we are empowered to do the work of healing and restoration, which in itself is a form of adoration.

But our adoration doesn't just fortify us; it also fortifies Black Madonna! Throughout history, Black Madonna's Black body has been attacked by white people who insist that Black Madonna isn't really Black. Instead, they claim that she is actually white but has been darkened over the years by the soot from the thousands of candles that pilgrims light in devotion to her. They claim that Black Madonnas are simply highly venerated white Virgin Marys that are especially known for their miraculous powers. According to their claim, it was only through her worship (e.g., pilgrims lighting candles at their altar) that Black Madonna became black in color. Of course, this claim is rooted in anti-Blackness and an incapacity to imagine Black divinity, and can be easily debunked. (For example, why aren't Black Madonna's gowns, which in many cases are worn continuously for years at a time, also soiled by the candle soot?) But in a sly intellectual exercise, Thompson temporarily entertained this preposterous assertion in order to raise an important question: "What does it mean for an object to become Black through excessive worship and to have that very Blackness and its association with fertility, be that which produces even more veneration resulting in even more Blackness?" In other words, Thompson masterfully subverts their anti-Black claim and uses it to affirm Black Madonna's powerful Blackness. "So what you're saying is that Black Madonna is Black because so many people have worshipped her. And the more she is worshipped, the Blacker she gets. And the Blacker she gets, the more powerful she becomes. And the more powerful she becomes, the more people worship her. And the cycle continues . . ."[11]

Though we know Black Madonna is Black because she is in the lineage of the ancient Sacred Black Feminine, the original Mother of Africa, Thompson's point is well taken and demonstrates the beautiful mutuality between Black Madonna and her people. For our adoration does in fact affirm and expand her power and deepen her Blackness. As a profoundly relational deity, Black Madonna's power expands through her people. When we practice adoration, we fortify ourselves and ignite hope in our communities. In doing so, we expand Black Madonna's power—for we are her body and she often works miracles through us. And as more of us are transformed by our adoration, more of us become true Black Madonna kin and the colors of the rainbow that are represented in her Blackness increase. Yes, our adoration does make her Blacker—and the Blacker she gets, the more powerful she becomes. Yes. Yes. Yes!

FROM MIRACLE-HARVESTING TO MIRACLE-SEEKING

Truly embodying Black Madonna as we seek restorative healing in our communities is our deepest desire. Yet it is the miracle we are most afraid to seek. As privileged Americans who have been conditioned by an unreliable and petulant white patriarchal god, we have stopped looking to the Divine for help and have settled for a miracle-less spirituality. Over years of white patriarchal conditioning, we have repeatedly and painfully learned that this god is disinterested at best and actively fueling our pain at worst. We know that this god is *not* on the side of the oppressed and will not respond to our cries for help. So rather than seeking miracles, we arm ourselves with the finite weapons of colonialism and try to make miracles happen on our own. It's easier to forget about the possibility of divine rescue than risk yet another heartbreak from a deadbeat father god who claims to love us. When we are disillusioned, cynical, and armed only with the weapons of colonialism, vulnerably asking the Divine for a miracle becomes impossible.

In the midst of ongoing oppression and divine abandonment, we have forgotten the deeper truth that the ancient Sacred Black Feminine, the fierce cannonball-catchin' Black Madonna, perpetually offers us her cosmic breast milk and patiently waits for us to seek it, drink it, and embody the miracles for which we long. Because we have lost touch with our Infinite Mother who eagerly responds to our most pressing and vulnerable needs, we have lost touch with our most pressing and vulnerable needs too. As anyone who grew up in a neglectful home can attest, when our needs go unmet for far too long, we begin to deny that we have any needs at all. Rather than connecting with our deepest, most vulnerable needs and asking Black Madonna to miraculously intervene, we take on the much less daunting and risky task of expressing gratitude for the things she does even when we don't ask. In other words, many of us who are devoted to Black Madonna engage in the practice of miracle-harvesting rather than miracle-seeking. Miracle-harvesting is when we rightfully give her credit for the ways she, without solicitation, nourishes abundance in our lives, such as the soothing sound of rushing water, unconditional love, and unexpected but delightful surprises.

To be clear, miracle-harvesting is a glorious practice. It allows us to awaken to Black Madonna's incredible omnipresence in our lives. But the most powerful alchemy is in the miracle-seeking, not the miracle-harvesting. Miracle-harvesting is safe; we don't have to connect with our deepest need, nor honestly share it with Black Madonna. But when we honestly admit to ourselves and Black Madonna our most vulnerable needs, we create space for her to lovingly assure us (yet again) that she is the Mother of Miracles.

As we travel Black Madonna's spiritual path, we are invited to put down the weapons of colonialism that we think we need, release our hardened cynicism, and discover the intimacy of a truly vulnerable and trusting relationship with the Divine. But it all starts with the ancestral practice of adoration. Adoration begets hope, hope begets vulnerability, and vulnerability begets miracle-seeking. Adoration infuses us with the hope we need to ask boldly and vulnerably for miracles. When we are cloaked in Black Madonna's armor of adoration, our hope is fortified and we are emboldened to present our most authentic needs. With Black Madonna guiding us, it's just a matter of time before we begin to experience miracles beyond our ancestors' wildest imaginations.

ADORATION AND MIRACLE-SEEKING

Remember, O most gracious Virgin Mary, that never was it known that anyone who fled to thy protection, implored thy help, or sought thy intercession was left unaided. Inspired with this confidence, I fly to thee, O Virgin of virgins, my Mother; to thee do I come . . .
— **ANCIENT MEMORARE PRAYER**

Grounding

- *Reflect:* What is your body telling you today? Is there anything (e.g., beliefs, emotions, pain, ease, anxiety) that is hyper-present? What are your emotions describing? If it's easier, tune in to your bodily sensations and ask what story they are telling you today.

- *Express:* Write an honest letter to Black Madonna and tell her how you are showing up and what you are experiencing today.

Adoration

- *Reflect:* What gifts have you already received from Black Madonna? Some possible areas to consider: physical healing, spiritual awakening and empowerment, emotional healing, identity liberation, freedom to live/relate/hope/dream differently, tangible resources

- *Express:* Write an honest letter to Black Madonna and express any gratitude and adoration you have for her. If you'd like to go deeper, create a simple ex-voto in honor of your gratitude and adoration. An ex-voto can take any form, but here are some possible ideas to consider: plant seeds, bulbs, or a small tree; create a collage out of magazine or newspaper clippings; or make a drawing or painting (it doesn't have to look professional!).

Longing

- *Reflect:* Where are you longing for wholeness, protection, accompaniment, healing, breakthrough and/or a miracle, personally or in a broader community? In other words, where are you experiencing dis-ease in your life today and how are you longing for something different? Some possible areas to consider: uncertainty, loneliness, tangible need, physical or mental challenges, hopelessness, societal liberation, a shift in governmental and/or community leadership, an end to war, or support and freedom for a particular social group. Another way to think about it is: What do you hope to feel—emotionally, mentally, spiritually, and physically—as a result of the miracle you seek? What do you hope to experience in your body and in the world?

- *Express:* Grounding yourself in the recognition of the gifts you've already received from Black Madonna, write an honest letter to Black Madonna and directly express any longing, needs, or hopes that you are carrying.

Listen, Observe, and Receive

Take a few moments to listen to Black Madonna's response, keeping an open mind and expectant posture. She may directly speak to you verbally, or she may send a message via a human, an animal, an image, a quote, a song that comes to mind, or even an experience (such as physical healing or unexpectedly encountering a rock in the shape of a heart while you're on your daily walk). Or she may simply infuse you with a sensation or emotion that offers you the assurance and guidance you need for today.

If you don't perceive a response immediately, take heart: Remember that the Memorare prayer promises that a response is en route, and remain on the lookout in the coming hours and days. Black Madonna will surprise you, probably when you least expect it. And her response will be beautiful, dramatic, and beyond your wildest imagination.

8
INVOCATION

Mother of Us All,

You Leave Absolutely No One Behind.

Queen who loves people more than power,

You covet connection more than jewels.

You declare again and again that the most marginalized—

Indigenous kin who languish under the colonizer's heel,

Disabled people excluded from society's embrace,

Black trans folks who defy religious orthodoxy—

These are the ones you call your own.

Each night you claim them when you leave your fancy basilica,

The one that the powerful insiders built for you,

To walk in the lowly fields with your beloved outsiders.

Anoint us with the moral courage to walk with you too.

Mother of Us All,

You Leave Absolutely No One Behind.

Your infinite Blackness blooms in all beings,

You encounter yourself in every single one of us,

Even those we foolishly deem godless.

Your mercy is a surgical knife.

You expose our hard hearts,

Then softly suture them with love.

Yes, even your rage is compassionate.

When you confront evil, you do it your way:

Restoration over retribution,

Sacredness over sanctimony.

Anoint our eyes to seek you in each face too.

Mother of Us All,

You Leave Absolutely No One Behind.

Like us, you know the angst of deferred hope,

The heartbreak of ashes, the grief of stolen justice.

Amid setbacks and stymied liberation,

Refurbish our hearts, recondition our souls.

Make us mystic-activists with vision to see

That your body is the arc of the universe.

Insure us and assure us with your vast cosmic plan,

That though long, your body's arc bends toward love.

Transform us, release us to fully trust you.

Anoint us with hope to ride you toward love too.

Chapter 8

SHE ANOINTS US TO EMBODY HER IN THE WORLD

Empowered by Black Madonna Who Leaves Absolutely *No One* Behind

If the famed fashion house Dolce&Gabbana had a matron saint, I bet it would be the fabulous Filipina Black Madonna of Piat. Much like the designers at Dolce&Gabbana, the Black Madonna of Piat seems to embody the maximalist maxim that "more is more." When it comes to style, Black Madonnas are a diverse bunch. Some, like the pregnant and barefoot Black Madonna of Mende, are humbly dressed in what could be mistaken for a potato sack. A few—such as the Black Madonna of Paris, who wears a simple but beautiful red, white, and blue robe—dress so much like Renaissance-era commoners that they could have walked the streets incognito. Others—like the Black Madonna of Montserrat, with her timeless, unembellished golden robe—are tailored in an understated yet elegant manner, as if Coco Chanel is their stylist. Still others take bling to a cosmic level and make it holy. The Black Madonna of Piat is a member of this Sisterhood of the Holy Bling.

In a deeply Catholic country, the Black Madonna of Piat is one of the most venerated images of the Virgin Mary, and her holy bling confirms her elevated status among other Filipina Marys. Seeing her so often adorned in a rich hue of royal blue and dazzling gold, one can't help but notice her exquisite glamour. Many Black Madonnas are made of wood or stone, but the life-sized Black Madonna of Piat is unique in that she is composed of papier-mâché. As a result, she looks more like an alluring department store mannequin than a traditional religious statue. Eyebrows arched, dramatic eyelashes affixed to her eyelids, lips pursed, and bronzer generously applied to her cheeks—she looks like she just stopped by the MAC counter for a quick glow-up, *because why not?*

But her clothing and accessories are the real showstoppers. Enrobed in satin lined with overlapping golden braids and lace and covered with complex patterns of embroidered roses, tulips, and leaves, the Black Madonna of Piat is perpetually red carpet–ready. Atop her head sits an enormous, multitier crown adorned with just about every fine gem you can imagine: diamonds, rubies, sapphire, emeralds, and more. And the diamond chandelier earrings dangling from her dainty earlobes look so expensive, they should have their own security detail.

As far as I'm concerned, this is plenty of holy bling, but clearly the Black Madonna of Piat disagrees. Her holy bling continues with two large concentric halos—one made of gold and embedded with rubies and the other made of silver and embedded with diamonds—framing her head and torso. Each glitzy halo is lined with scores of what, at first glance, look like pointy metallic stars.

When I first saw them, I thought, *Sure, halos lined with stars seems on-brand for this wonderfully glamorous Black Madonna. With her, more is definitely more!*

But as I learned more about the Black Madonna of Piat, I discovered that the "stars" are actually burrs from the amorseco plant—a plant that is common in the region of the Philippines that is heavily populated by the Itawis and Ibanag peoples.

Herein lies the theological genius of the Black Madonna of Piat. Her opulence, showstopping fashion, and jewels suggest that she is all about money, appearance, and that exclusive rich life. But the amorseco burrs tell another story and are the key to understanding who the Black Madonna of Piat really is, who she really stands with and for, and what she's really all about.

The Itawis and Ibanag tribes are some of the oldest Indigenous groups in the Philippines, and many members still proudly bear the dark mahogany skin that many Filipinos had before the country was colonized and whitened by Spain. Additionally, both tribes are extreme ethnic minorities in the Philippines. In a country of almost 110 million people, Itawis number only 229,000 and Ibanags make up only 463,390 people.[1] Like many other Indigenous people around the globe, the dark-skinned Itawis and Ibanags face ongoing colorism, discrimination, and dehumanization, including a horrific epidemic of missing and murdered women and girls.[2]

Agricultural tribes, the Itawis and Ibanag gravitate toward the rural areas in the Cagayan River Valley in northeastern Philippines and spend most of their days in the fields planting, nurturing, and harvesting rice, corn, peanuts, legumes, and root crops.[3] Since the fields are full of amorseco plants with pesky burrs that stick to clothing, an Itawi or Ibanag farmer is typically covered in burrs by the end of the work day. Clothes adorned with amorseco burrs are a key marker of the Itawis and Ibanag people, especially the farmers and field laborers, who often experience the most economic oppression and other forms of marginalization.

The Black Madonna of Piat wears these burrs too.

In a country of over 76 million Catholics,[4] the Black Madonna of Piat, who is arguably the most famous and powerful Virgin Mary in the land, wears the burrs of an extremely marginalized and oppressed group of dark-skinned, Indigenous Filipinos.

The burrs on this Black Madonna's halos, as well as the many burrs that are also embroidered on her robes, signify her solidarity with the marginalized Itawis and Ibanags, who represent less than one percent of the Catholic population. According to Filipino monk and church historian Brother Aaron Veloso, the Itawis and Ibanag people fervently believe that despite Black Madonna's queenly bling and primary residence in the relatively fancy basilica in Piat, she loves them so much that every evening she walks among the fields in order to be with them.[5] Anybody who walks in the fields with the Itawis and Ibanag people is going to find themselves covered in amorseco burrs. Because the Black Madonna of Piat walks the fields with her people, it's only natural that her clothing and accessories would also be covered in burrs.

To the Itawis and Ibanag people, Black Madonna's splendor doesn't diminish her ability to connect with them, on their turf, in their fields. They know that they don't have to travel all the way to the fancy basilica in the city, nor do they have to clean themselves up and adorn themselves with ornate clothes in order to be embraced by her. The Itawis and Ibanags know that the blingy Black Madonna of Piat loves to get down and dirty in their lives, that she'll go to any length to express her love and protection for them. They know that she will come to them, even though it means walking through fields full of pesky burrs.

The Itawis and Ibanags also understand that she is not ashamed of their dark skin. As a Black Madonna with naturally dark skin, she is one of them. In a society maligned with colorism, she claims her dark skin and stands among the dark-skinned Itawis and Ibanag people. And like them, her radiantly dark skin is made even darker by her time in the fields with them. She is kissed by the sun, and her melanated skin shimmers with darkness, just like theirs.

The Itawis and Ibanags understand that, unlike much of colonial Filipino society, their beloved Black Madonna is not embarrassed to be associated with them—for she does not remove her burrs, the evidence that she has spent time with them, before she returns to her basilica. Rather, she proudly dons the burrs and even elevates them into fine adornments for all to behold. She takes the burrs, a symbol of marginalization, and makes them high fashion. In doing so she proclaims, "Their burrs are my jewels. The very characteristics you despise in the precious people who bear these burrs are the same characteristics that I cherish. I cherish the dark skin that you denigrate. I cherish the missing women and children that you ignore. I stand in solidarity with the struggle for justice with which you cannot be bothered." In fact, the Black Madonna of Piat holds an ornate hanky in her hand, and the Itawis believe this to be a symbol of her tears on behalf of their plight.

By wearing the burrs as holy bling, Black Madonna is inviting us to see the most marginalized people of the world as she sees them, and embrace them as she embraces them. Her holy bling shimmers and sparkles and catches our eyes and turns our heads toward her. Her gorgeous makeup and intricately embroidered clothing beckon us close, so that when we're near enough and she has our undivided attention, she can show us who she's really here for and what she's really about.

Make no mistake: though she loves her bling, she loves her people more. She'll happily ruin a haute couture gown if that means she gets to walk in the fields with her cherished children. The people—especially the Itwawis, Ibanags, and other marginalized peoples—are her real treasures. If we really want to seek her, we needn't look for her in the basilica. If we really want to commune with her, we must venture into the fields and labor among the people whom society has taught us to despise. If we really want to embody her, we too must clothe ourselves in burrs.

The Black Madonna of Piat's official Church title is Our Lady of the Visitation, which likely refers to her practice of visiting the Itawis and Ibanags in their burr-filled fields. However, the Ibanag people have a special name for her in their language: Yena Tam Ngamin, which means "Mother of Us All" in English.[6] They understand that the fact she eagerly embraces them, the lowest on the Filipino societal ladder, means that she eagerly embraces all of us. For if she embraces and affirms the sacredness of the most marginalized and ostracized, then she embraces and affirms all of us. Indeed, she is the Mother of Us All.

BLACK MADONNA CONSISTENTLY STANDS WITH THE MARGINALIZED

In many ways Black Madonna is full of intrigue and difficult to predict. For example, she can be found in a variety of places and spaces: sometimes she makes her home in ornate cathedrals, and sometimes she happily abides in roadside hovels. Additionally, as we discovered in Chapter 6, since Black Madonna is queen of the fire, her practice of destroying in order to nurture new life can seem very befuddling to the human mind. Further, her tactical responses to conflict and oppression can be somewhat unpredictable. Most of the time, she employs cunning diplomacy or subversive workarounds in order to protect, nourish, and liberate her people. But stories about the Black Madonna of Paris (aka Our Lady of Fuck Around and Find Out) disappearing abusive husbands, like the story we encountered in Chapter 1, emphasize that she isn't afraid to use force if she deems it necessary in a particular situation. These examples remind us that Black Madonna's vast and complex Blackness cannot be entirely understood or predicted by the human mind. Though her end goal is always restorative love, in most cases there's really no telling what Black Madonna is going to do or how she is going to show up. We often wait on her with bated breath, ready to follow her lead no matter what she asks of us or where she takes us.

Yet Black Madonna is remarkably consistent when it comes to demonstrating her unrelenting preference for the marginalized. No matter the era or location, in every interpersonal power dynamic and in every oppressive conflict or war, Black Madonna powerfully reveals herself as a divine being who identifies and stands with the underdogs. The stories of Black Madonna advocating for, allying herself with, and empowering the most marginalized are endless.

From 1981 to 1989, in the years leading up to the Rwandan genocide of 1994, the Black Madonna of Kibeho regularly appeared to the people of Rwanda. Each time, she conveyed a powerful message of love and urged the relatively powerful Hutu tribe, who had been colonially conditioned to denigrate and oppress the relatively disempowered Tutsi tribe, to release their hatred. During her hundreds of appearances, the Black Madonna of Kibeho issued "dire, apocalyptic warnings that hatred . . . would lead Rwanda and the rest of the world into a dark abyss."[7] *Years* before human experts such as political scientists, global leaders, and diplomats were even aware of the problem, the Black Madonna of Kibeho was standing in solidarity with the Tutsis, raising the alarm about the impending genocide, and working to restore beloved community in Rwanda.

Just a few years earlier, at the height of the South African anti-apartheid movement and while Nelson Mandela was still imprisoned at Robben Island, Black Madonna took up residence in the Regina Mundi Catholic Church in Soweto. The largest township in South Africa, Soweto is home to more than 2 million Black people who live in cramped and often squalid conditions. When Black Madonna chose Soweto as her home and became known as the Black Madonna of Soweto, she proclaimed her identification with the most marginalized and resoundingly affirmed that Black life is holy, despite the colonial apartheid government's strenuous attempts to denigrate it. As South African theologian Michelle Wolff explains, the Black Madonna of Soweto "points to the harm committed against Black South Africans generally and Soweto residents specifically . . . intimat[ing] the far more radical notion that God sanctions the life and prosperity of Black South Africans over and against apartheid."[8] Not surprisingly, this Black Madonna became a significant icon of resistance in the anti-apartheid movement. Since all public meetings except church gatherings were outlawed by the apartheid government, many anti-apartheid meetings were surreptitiously held in Black Madonna's church, and she became known as a powerful source of liberation. Later in the 1990s, Bishop Desmond Tutu held many of the now-famous Truth and Reconciliation Commission meetings at her church, under her watchful eye.

The Black Madonnas of Kibeho and Soweto powerfully demonstrate that whether the conflict is intertribal or interracial, Black Madonna stands with the most oppressed and advocates for a world of equitable unity. But she isn't just concerned about the people who experience economic, tribal, and racial oppression; she's deeply concerned about people who experience gender and sexual oppression as well. Not surprisingly, Black Madonna began advocating for her LGBTQIA kin centuries before even the most progressive religious groups became aware of their exclusionary practices.

The Black Madonna of Montevergine has been known for centuries as a divine being who represents, protects, and stands with transgender people. This glorious Black Madonna is the most powerful in the Campania region of southern Italy and is a modern Sacred Black Feminine iteration of the ancient supergoddess Cybele. According to research by Alessandra Belloni, "Historically, men who wanted to be initiated in the mysteries of Cybele became women through a ritual castration. . . . They were known as Galli, and as priestesses they played the frame drums and danced in ecstasy."[9] Today, the *femminielli* (nonbinary/transgender Italians) continue this drumming and dancing tradition of the worship of Black Madonna. Throughout the years, the Black Madonna of Montevergine has demonstrated that though she embraces all people, she especially loves LGBTQIA people.[10] In 1256, two gay lovers were expelled from their village, tied to a tree in the winter forest, and left to die. However, Black Madonna came to their rescue, untied them, and brought them into her church to live. Each year on Candlemas (February 2), there is a huge LGBTQIA processional to the monastery in Montevergine followed by a pride celebration, and this powerful spiritual event has also made a political impact. For example, Ospedaletto d'Alpinolo, the city closest to the monastery, was the first city in Italy to open a gender-neutral restroom, in 2017.

Even when oppressive powers appropriate Black Madonna and weaponize her against the most marginalized, she subverts the oppressive powers and makes her commitment to the marginalized resoundingly clear. For example, Christopher Columbus claimed to be a fervent devotee of Black Madonna. He actually believed that his colonial and genocidal actions were ordained by her and an act of worship of her. Case in point: Columbus named the Caribbean islands of Guadeloupe and Montserrat after two famous Black Madonnas in Spain. Columbus is proof that simply switching our deity or divine archetype isn't going to heal our internalized patriarchy. Colonialism and white patriarchy are shape-shifters; they can morph into and weaponize just about anything. If we don't deal with them at the root, our so-called devotion to Black Madonna will simply be devotion to a blackface version of the white patriarchal god.

But there's good news! If a powerful archetype like Black Madonna can be misappropriated and weaponized, then it can also be reclaimed and transformed. In his incredible book *Our Lady of Class Struggle: The Cult of the Virgin Mary in Haiti*, sociologist Terry Rey affirms, "Whatever the interests that European imperialism intended to promote through the symbol of the Virgin Mary in the colony, religiously heretical and politically resistant groups have . . . effectively transformed the mother of Jesus from a legitimizing force for the slave regime into an oppositional form of religious capital that met under-class religious needs and served under-class political interests."[11] We see this unfold in full force in the birth story of the Haitian Revolution. When Napoleon hired Polish mercenaries to help the French army squelch the nascent revolution in Haiti, the Polish brought their devotion to the superpowerful Black Madonna of Częstochowa with them. But upon their arrival in Haiti, the Poles quickly surveyed the oppressive colonial conditions, realized that Napoleon (not the Haitians) was the real threat, and betrayed Napoleon by siding with the Haitians *against* the French. While fighting in solidarity with the Haitians, the mercenaries introduced the people to their Black Madonna of Częstochowa, who was readily adopted by the Haitian people as their own mother and advocate. They incorporated her into the pantheon of Vodou spirits as Erzulie Dantor, a fierce protector of women and children—and she became a powerful force behind the Haitian Revolution.

Black Madonna is wonderfully subversive in this way. Even when white patriarchy thinks it is in control, Black Madonna works with the people to nurture life and liberation, no matter the physical reality. When bell hooks urged Black people to "reclaim the Black Madonna as an icon of resistance," I think this is what she meant. But in order to enact Black Madonna's restorative, matriarchal version of justice, we must learn to identify and heal from our internalized patriarchy.

EMBODYING THE MOTHER OF US ALL: CHOOSING RESTORATION OVER RETRIBUTION, SACREDNESS OVER SANCTIMONY

In the medieval town of Arras, a married woman was boiling over with rage. You see, she had recently discovered that her merchant husband had started sleeping with another woman in their small village. In such a robustly patriarchal society, it's no surprise that the man was not held accountable for his actions. Rather, the women bore the burden of his toxic masculinity–induced sexual escapades. Naturally, in a society where wives had very little power in a marriage, the troubled and infuriated wife began to question her own stability and point accusatory fingers at the husband's mistress. As if it were a *Real Housewives of Arras* reality TV episode, the wife publicly shamed the mistress. Naturally, the mistress didn't love being thrashed in the center of the town square and summarily rebuffed the wife. So, as the story goes, the two women "without exaggeration, were at each other's throats," with little hope of restoration, according to 13th-century historian and King Alfonso X of Castile, León and Galicia, who recorded this tale.[12]

Frustrated and vengeful, one night before bed the woman pleaded with Black Madonna, asking her to throw every ounce of sorrow and pain toward the mistress "because it was she who made her lose the great pleasure she once had of her husband."[13]

But that night while the woman slept, Black Madonna appeared to her in a dream saying, "I have heard your prayer but it is not my way nor does it please me to be cruel. What is more, that woman goes to kneel at my altar and gives thanks to me a hundred times a day, bowing her head to the ground."[14]

The story doesn't include details about what the woman said or felt in response to this dream—but if it were me, and if I'm being honest, I imagine that I might be infuriated.

"*That woman* thinks she can mess with my man and then go to the church and kneel before my Black Madonna in pious prayer? What a hypocrite! This is all the more reason why she should burn in hell," I might sear and seethe.

I imagine I might also feel betrayed by Black Madonna and work to manipulate her into siding with me.

"*Don't you see* that I am being wronged and that you should be on *my* side and that you should be *against* that horrible woman? *Clearly*, I'm the better person here," I might argue and gloat.

But Black Madonna was up to something.

When the wife awoke the next morning, she went out to the street and the mistress was there waiting for her. Without hesitation, the mistress knelt before the woman, confessed her wrongdoing, and affirmed, "I will do it no more, as it grieves you."

No longer defensive, the mistress acknowledged the wife's pain, owned her harmful behavior, and promised to never do it again. In response, the wife softened her heart toward the mistress and stepped off her moral pedestal, and the two were reconciled.

Who knows what Black Madonna said to the mistress in order to compel her to stop participating in harm and to make things right? And who knows what Black Madonna said to the wife in order to soften her heart toward the mistress and put down her vindictive arrows? We simply know that Black Madonna did it her way, not either of the women's way.

This story highlights how the Mother of Us All does not leave anyone behind. Never vengeful, she is the essence of love, a love that has room for all of us. If we have willing hearts and follow her lead, she will take the messes we have made of our lives and compost them into true restorative justice. As we explored in Chapter 2, for millennia Black Madonna has been associated with the fierce and tender love of a lioness who licks her cubs into shape and life. Like a lioness, Black Madonna loved, withheld, prodded, and compelled the two women into a restorative relationship. In the face of late-stage capitalism, enduring colonialism, and an increasingly divided world, more than ever we need the fierce and tender love of Black Madonna. We need her to restore the parts of us that have been stricken and disempowered by white patriarchy. We need her to lick us into shape and life.

The Mother of Us All is inviting all of us to pause, take a deep breath, and ask ourselves, "What, exactly, is the justice we are seeking?" In other words, she is beckoning us into wholeness rather than vindication; restoration rather than retribution. Whether we are responding to interpersonal injustice, as are the women in this story, or to systemic oppression between groups of people, she's concerned about our entire well-being and the restoration of our entire community. Rather than seeking coerced compliance or the appearance of piety, she wants us to be free in every way—body, mind, and spirit. Rather than pronouncing one side victorious over the other, she carves a pathway to repair that leads to true unity upon her sacred and loving lap. As this story reveals, no matter how we have been harmed, she wants us to be free to embody our own sacredness while also affirming the sacredness of others—even those who harm us.

When I visited Palestine, a Muslim activist named Khaled told me that the heart of his spiritual practice is envisioning God in his Zionist enemies. He said that he spends hours each week affirming the sacredness of the very people who have tried to destroy his people because if he can no longer see God in his enemy, then he has already lost the fight for a free Palestine. This is the love that the Mother of Us All, who affirms the sacredness of all people, calls us to embody.

But it's worth noting that the Mother of Us All's supreme love is not devoid of accountability. Though our society often pits love and accountability against each other, Black Madonna knows better. There's something supernatural and distinctive about the way Black Madonna is able to simultaneously express unconditional love for you while also calling you out. Many of us who are raised in our white patriarchy–poisoned world have no concept of this mysterious concoction of love and accountability. For many, accountability only exists in the absence of love, whereas love is understood to be a conflict-free, "everything goes" zone. In fact, research on the pervasive culture of white patriarchy reveals that people who have been shaped by it tend to fall apart in the face of conflict precisely because the hierarchy of white patriarchy is designed to avoid conflict. So the beauty of someone lovingly but firmly calling you out is lost on many of us.

For example, many of us are shocked when we discover that though Harriet Tubman is credited with saving hundreds of enslaved Black people's lives, she wasn't afraid to threaten the lives of the Black people whose actions compromised the safety and wellness of the larger community. Once an escape attempt had begun, Harriet would threaten to shoot any escapee who tried to return to the plantation because their return would endanger the entire group. By threatening escapees in this way, she affirmed that they were sacred and deserved to freely journey with people who would not allow their personal fear to compromise the well-being of the group. Harriet's love for the community was so expansive that she confidently confronted anyone who intentionally or unintentionally harmed the group. Like Black Madonna, Harriet understood that love and accountability are two sides of the same sacred coin. As the stories about Our Lady of Fuck Around and Find Out (aka the Black Madonna of Paris) demonstrate, Black Madonna will forcefully banish people who persist in harming her loved ones and are unwilling to make amends. As the Mother of Us All, she is devoted to protecting the most vulnerable. She does not allow obstinate, remorseless people to indefinitely continue their harm.

Black Madonna's glorious marriage of love and accountability is on wonderful display in the medieval story of the wife and the mistress. Unlike a genie in a bottle, Black Madonna did more than simply respond to the unimaginative and vindictive prayers of the grieving wife. Instead, in her wisdom and grace, she restored the broken relationship between them, even if that meant refusing to give them what they thought they wanted. The opposite of a people-pleaser, Black Madonna violated the existing patriarchal norms and refused to crucify the mistress. But she held her accountable for her part in the harm. And though the wife's prayer was vindictive and cruel, Black Madonna didn't hold that against her. Instead she embraced the wife's humanity, listened intently to her prayer for help, and promptly responded in the most restorative way. In healing the relationship between the women, Black Madonna affirmed each woman's inherent dignity while calling both of them to a higher relationship—one that is full of both love *and* accountability.

Similarly, by embracing both love and accountability, Black Madonna did far more than restore an interpersonal relationship. She liberated two hurting women who were harmfully tethered to a system: patriarchy. By refusing to crucify the mistress but also lovingly calling her out, she affirmed the woman's sacredness and freed her to discover that she deserves more than the sexual scraps of an insecure and dishonest man. By responding to the wife's prayer but refusing to engage in cruelty, Black Madonna affirmed her sacredness by freeing her to discover that her wellness and stability can be found in her right relationships with other women in the community and not just in her marriage. By embodying both love and accountability, Black Madonna carved a pathway beyond interpersonal healing to freedom from systemic oppression.

Though she's outlived us all and has witnessed and experienced more horrors than we can possibly imagine, Black Madonna is not traumatized or reactive. In her endless wisdom and grace, she can deftly respond to injustice with deep wisdom rather than react in unchecked pain. We can trust her guidance as we navigate very complex and intersectional justice issues. For millennia she has spoken clearly to her people when they have asked for guidance, especially when they have asked her to help them respond to injustice and harm.

Speaking of injustice and harm, in true patriarchal fashion, the husband remains absent from this story. We can't know for sure whether he too is invited into the love and accountability of Black Madonna. But given that the two women he harmed had reconciled, were getting free from patriarchy together, and were now following the lead of our mischievous, creative, and restorative Black Madonna, we can collectively imagine that the philandering husband was in for a rude awakening.

We don't need to be certain about what happened to the husband because we know one thing for certain: Karma is Black Madonna.

And as we will discover in the next few paragraphs, that's really all we need to know.

EMBODYING THE MOTHER OF US ALL: ENTRUSTING THE ARC OF THE UNIVERSE TO BLACK MADONNA

As a lifelong activist, I'm often asked if I believe Martin Luther King Jr.'s hopeful proclamation: that the arc of the universe is long but it bends toward justice. Though I long for such certainty, I honestly don't know if that is true. As a trained scientist, I'm painfully aware that there is very little evidence to suggest that Earth and its humans will survive long enough to fully experience the truth, repair, and restoration that are long overdue. When my perspective is entirely shaped by this reality, I find that my activism is rooted in fear rather than love. I find myself making decisions out of resource scarcity. And frankly, I find myself embodying a savior complex.

If I don't say it, it won't get said. So I speak up even when I do not possess the spiritual resources to speak truth without dishonoring the sacredness of the people I long to influence.

If I don't take a stand, no one will. So I chaotically fight battles on every front, with no strategy, wise stewardship of my unique gifts, or long-term sustainability.

If I don't defend them, they will not be defended. So I intervene in situations without ever asking if the people I claim to be defending actually want my "help."

With this mentality, the entire weight of the world is on *me* as I run furiously to and fro, from event to event, writing article after article ad nauseum, angrily shaming others onto *my* activism bandwagon, and generally living a life that suggests that I believe that burnout is a fruit of the spirit.

Oh, and I'm lonely—there's no room for Black Madonna in my self-imposed savior complex.

Can you relate?

Yet as a budding mystic, I know that there is another way to work toward equity and restoration in this overwhelmingly oppressive world. I have discovered that I am a much softer, kinder, and more loving person when I manage to embrace the belief that though the reverberating clangs of oppression, war, and exploitation seem the loudest, love remains at the heart of reality. I am a much more creative and resilient person when my activism is rooted in the belief that love will ultimately shower us with exuberant anthems of equity, the perfect pitch of true healing, and the sweet harmonies that are finally released when the systems of domination are fully dismantled. I am a much more collaborative and harmonious person when, like the Kongolese revolutionaries at Stono, I am convinced that Black Madonna is guiding me and others into true freedom. I am a much more gracious and generous person when I embody the notion that in the end, love will win. I am a much more courageous and resilient person when, like bell hooks, I experience Black Madonna as an icon of resistance who can transform how the world sees Black women and truly all people.

More and more, I want my justice efforts to spring from the eternal well of mysticism rather than my barren savior complex. Of course, this is easier said than done; when we are daily confronted with the hard evidence of oppression, hope seems like a fantasy from a universe far, far away. But when I recount the jaw-dropping story of the little-known Black Madonna of Meillers, France, hope seems closer to Earth. When I take refuge in the story of this particular Black Madonna, the clamor of fear slowly dims and I begin to experience what Arundhati Roy once proclaimed: "Another world is not only possible, she is on her way. On a quiet day, I can hear her breathing."[15] When I embrace the Black Madonna of Meillers, I discover with relief that all along, the ancient Sacred Black Feminine has been guiding us through the ups and downs of the long but restorative arc of the universe. The Black Madonna of Meillers is the one I return to again and again when I find that I need to release the weight of the world to the time-tested and trustworthy Sacred Black Feminine.

I first learned of the universe-bearing Black Madonna of Meillers in 2023 during my annual pilgrimage to the Auvergne region of central France, where I spend several weeks a year communing with the numerous ancient Black Madonnas in the region. A couple of days into my trip, my Airbnb host, Bérengère, called me from happy hour, her voice brimming with excitement. With the clanging of cocktail glasses and the soft buzz of conversation in the background, Bérengère explained that a friend had just told her about an ancient Black Madonna from the tiny village of Meillers, about an hour's drive from where I was staying, who had recently experienced an incredible miracle!

"I don't have to work on Saturday. Do you want me to take you to go see this Black Madonna?" Bérengère generously offered.

I had never heard of the Black Madonna of Meillers, but of course I said yes! In the ensuing days, I read several local news articles about this mysterious Black Madonna and learned that she dates to the 12th century and has made her home in the humble village church of Meillers, which is about an hour's drive from Clermont-Ferrand, my "hometown" when I am on pilgrimage in central France. Though Meillers is situated in the idyllic countryside and surrounded by peaceful winding roads and soft rolling hills, this Black Madonna's history is anything *but* idyllic, peaceful, and soft.

Like many Black Madonnas, she and her child were stolen and presumed destroyed during the French Revolution. Then in 1850 she was discovered alone in a barrel of ashes, her child nowhere to be found. As we know from the stories of the Black Madonna of Einsiedeln, Black Madonna is legendary for being the sole survivor of an otherwise all-consuming fire. So it's no surprise that the 19th-century citizens of Meillers assumed that all that remained of the child was ashes. They built a new child when they were happily reunited with their beloved Madonna. But they always knew that the child was simply a stand-in and that their Mother was still tragically separated from her true child. In fact, in 1907 when the ancient Black Madonna was designated a national historical monument, the replacement child was excluded from the honor. As if being a prisoner of war, languishing in a barrel of ashes, and being separated from her cosmic child as well as her human children in the village of Meillers for over 50 years were not enough, calamity again befell in 2007 when Black Madonna and her replacement child were targeted and stolen by a thief who specialized in sacred object heists. She and the replacement child were eventually recovered 200 miles away in Paris and returned to Meillers. Throughout this entire ordeal, Black Madonna remained separated from her true child.

Then, in early 2023, a miracle occurred! A well-known antique dealer named Bernard Vassy was conducting a routine estate inventory for a recently deceased Clermont-Ferrand couple. Among the ho-hum antiques, Bernard encountered a strange and exquisite statue of a Christ child. Bernard didn't recognize the child, but he knew it was special and worth investigating, so rather than putting it up for auction, he alerted the French Union of Professional Experts in Works of Art and Collectibles. After examining it, they confirmed that it was the long-lost child of the Black Madonna of Meillers.

After learning this incredible backstory, I was even more excited to visit the magical Black Madonna of Meillers, who was reunited with her precious child after more than 225 years apart. I couldn't wait to gaze into the eyes of a Black mother who understood what it was like to lose her son to systemic violence and to hope for years and years that he was somehow, somewhere out there and safe. I couldn't wait to pray to the holy Black mother who understood the pain of riding the seemingly endless arc of the universe, hoping that at some point, she will encounter restoration and reunion. I couldn't wait to commune with the Sacred Black Feminine who could empathize with my pain of encountering yet another act of violence while I still waited for healing from the previous bout of violence. I longed to embrace the Black Madonna of Meillers, whose very body is the arc of the universe—sometimes present, sometimes stolen, sometimes surrounded by ashes, sometimes separated from her beloved, but *always* moving toward hope and restoration. I couldn't wait to light a candle in gratitude to the dark wooden Black Madonna whose mystical story silences the clamor of fear so that, like Arundhati Roy, I can hear the other possible world that is on her way.

As promised, the next Saturday, a sunny December afternoon, Bérengère picked me up and we began following the winding roads toward Meillers. After about an hour of cheerful and hopeful chatting, we finally arrived at the simple stone church. As we entered the empty sanctuary, I made a beeline for the front altar, where Black Madonnas in village churches often hold court. But all I encountered was an empty statue pedestal encased in a clear, bulletproof box.

Where was she? Had she been stolen again? *Or did the village keep her locked away because they were afraid that she'll be stolen again?*

Bérengère and I were perplexed, so we exited the church and crossed the country road to the village's lone restaurant. Inside we inquired about the Vierge Noire, and the hostess told us she didn't know where she was but that we could ask the mayor, who lived just down the street. So off we went to the mayor's house and knocked on the door. As an American who loves a good boundary, I was reluctant to bug the mayor . . . on a Saturday . . . at her house. But Bérengère didn't seem to share my concerns and banged loudly on the old wooden door. The mayor didn't seem at all perturbed when she opened the door and encountered two strangers asking about the town's Vierge Noire. In fact, the mayor seemed honored and excited to recant the miraculous story to us! But when we asked where, exactly, we could see the incredible Black Madonna of Meillers, the mayor informed us that she is in a special lab being prepared to be reunited with her child. You see, because Black Madonna had been separated from her child for over 225 years, they were each accustomed to very different levels of humidity. If they were hastily reunited, they would harm each other because their wood had lived in very different environments for over two centuries. So in preparation for their long-awaited reunion, they were each undergoing a nine-month reconditioning process in which they were slowly being introduced to increasingly similar levels of humidity. The goal is that when they are finally reunited, they will experience true unity without harming each other.

As I listened to the mayor, I audibly gasped. I couldn't believe that after all these years, the long-suffering Black Madonna had to wait even longer. My heart felt so much compassion for her because I too know what it means to wait and wait and wait for the healing and restoration for which I long. And yet, something about the story unlocked a mystical secret too. If the Black Madonna of Meillers, the arc of the universe herself, chooses to ride the arc a little bit longer because she knows that haste can cause harm, then that makes her even more trustworthy as we wait and hope.

When we entrust the arc of the universe to Black Madonna, everything changes.

We wait and hope and continue our efforts toward healing and restoration knowing that her timeline, though perplexing to our human minds, just may be protecting us from further harm. We wait and hope and continue our efforts toward healing and restoration knowing that her timeline just may be preventing us from prematurely conjuring a fake child when our souls truly long for the real deal. We wait and hope and continue our efforts toward healing and restoration knowing that our anguish is not dismissed by her, for she too rides the arc with us and has experienced our languishing ups and downs. We wait and hope and continue our efforts toward healing and restoration knowing that her timeline, though befuddling to us, is right on time. We wait and hope and continue our efforts toward healing and restoration knowing that we can release control to the arc of the universe herself, for she loves us dearly and is going to make sure that true reunion happens.

I've noticed that some activists possess a certain quality that's hard to put a finger on; you just know it when you see it. They are generous and grounded, they are hopeful even when the situation seems hopeless, they are gracious even toward their "enemies," and their powerful convictions are reflected not just in their speech but in their embodied lives. Theologian Curtiss DeYoung calls these exemplary humans "mystic-activists" and defines them as people driven by an activism that consumes them but is "deeply rooted in their faith and in the mystery of the divine."[16] According to DeYoung, activism that taps into the infinite creativity and limitless regeneration of the sacred is the kind of activism that can nurture the fierce and visionary hope that fuels resilient justice leadership. Building upon DeYoung's wonderful definition, I would add that mystic-activists are people who fully relinquish control of the outcome while still exerting every great effort toward the work of healing and restoration. Even when the times feel extremely urgent, we can entrust the arc of the universe to the Black Madonna of Meillers and root ourselves in her trustworthiness as we take courageous steps toward healing and restoration.

Though the Black Madonna of Meillers story nourishes many activist pathways, it feels particularly well attuned to the issue of climate crisis, which lands most violently on the bodies of Black and brown people. The times truly are urgent as the arc of the universe appears to be coming to a catastrophic end. Yet geologist Marcia Bjornerud, who is greatly concerned about the fate of our planet, cautions against an ungrounded sense of urgency that consumes us when we don't root our climate crisis efforts in a profound understanding of Earth's ancient history. According to Bjornerud, if we move too hastily, we can cause greater harm to our planet even as we seek to heal it. For example, she notes that since large volcanic eruptions temporarily pause global warming, many climate crisis thought leaders have advocated for "the injection of reflective sulfate aerosol particles into the stratosphere—the upper atmosphere—to mimic the effect of large volcanic eruptions . . ." In other words, they want to chemically induce volcanic reactions in order to halt global warming. It sounds like a brilliant and relatively cheap idea! But Bjornerud cautions against this artificial "quick fix" because "even small changes to intricate natural systems can have large and unanticipated consequences." Instead she recommends grounding all climate change efforts in what she calls "timefulness," "a clear-eyed view of our place in Time, both the past that came along before us and the future that will elapse without us." When she is operating from timefulness, Bjornerud writes, "I am comforted by the knowledge that we live on a very old, durable planet, not an immature, untested and possibly fragile one."[17] Even in the midst of an immense crisis, Bjornerud finds spaciousness in the long history and durability of Earth. From this belly of spaciousness, she is able to wisely collaborate with others in a way that doesn't succumb to fearful urgency.

Black Madonna, our primordial Earth Mother, the Sacred Black Feminine, the ancient one, is an old and time-tested deity. Even as we face urgent, painful, and seemingly hopeless realities, we can find spaciousness in the durability and resilience of Black Madonna. Despite all that she has experienced, she's still here and she's still embodying the arc of the universe that is long but bends toward love. As mystic-activists, we can put down our self-imposed savior complexes and ride the arc with her, knowing that she has thought of everything and that our reunion will be more than we've ever dreamed of.

THE MOST DECREPIT BLACK MADONNA EVER

The fierce Black Madonna of Moulins, the one to whom Joan of Arc prayed in 1429 before she went into battle, is only an hour's train ride from Clermont-Ferrand. During one of my frequent visits to Moulins, a café owner told me that the nearby village of Bresnay had an ancient Black Madonna. Despite my extensive research on the Black Madonnas of central France, I had never heard of this Black Madonna. In fact, I had never heard of Bresnay. This village, with a population of 300, is so small that it doesn't even have its own bakery.

But when I saw her pictures and read her story online, I knew I wanted to meet her.

The next week I returned to Moulins and set out for Bresnay (about 20 kilometers away). When I arrived at the town hall, where I was told I would find the ancient Black Madonna, the town clerk, Isabella, and I looked all over the storage areas but didn't find her. So Isabella started making calls (like, eight of them) and learned that this Black Madonna was kept in a tiny chapel about a 10-minute drive down the road. A woman in the village named Sylvie offered to pick me up and take me there. So off we went, with one of those big, old-timey keys.

When we arrived at the tiny countryside chapel, Black Madonna's chapel situation broke my heart! Even though she was in the chapel and under a roof, the cold weather, wood worms, and other elements had clearly taken a toll on her. I started to tear up when I noticed that her Black female body looks as weathered as my Black female body often feels.

But while we were there gazing at Black Madonna, my guide said that the statue in the chapel is actually a copy and that the original is safely stored in the town hall.

I was like, *"Wait, what*? I was just in the town hall, and she wasn't there."

So we got back in the car and returned to the town hall. And we got some more old-timey keys from the town key box and searched even more attic-y rooms and finally found the original Black Madonna in a room full of Christmas decorations. Voilà!

The original Black Madonna of Bresnay stood robustly, easefully, and confidently; her dark walnut-colored skin shined brightly. She looked spry, well rested, and ready to ignite a revolutionary fire. She looked like how I feel on the rare occasions that I receive enough support, affirmation, and guidance as a Black woman. I couldn't stop embracing her, perhaps because I implicitly understood that I can receive her rooted power by osmosis. Just being near her boosted my own energy levels and reminded me that a world in which all Black women are sacred and free is worth fighting for, no matter how many setbacks or impediments we encounter. The Black Madonna of Bresnay beams with "You're too sacred for this" energy. My encounter with the original, safely protected Black Madonna was so joyful that it felt like emotional whiplash in comparison to the sorrow I experienced in the presence of the weathered decoy Black Madonna. The juxtaposition between caring for and protecting Black women's bodies and not caring for and not protecting Black women's bodies was viscerally illustrated in the very different conditions of the original Black Madonna and her decoy.

Later, I randomly bumped into the mayor, Alain, and his wife, Michelle, at the village's lone market. Alain had already heard all about me via the town phone tree. On the spot, they invited me back to their meticulously restored 1700s French farmhouse for a tasty home-cooked lunch and savory green tea. I spent the entire afternoon lounging around their house, hearing about the village's history with their beloved Black Madonna, and enjoying wonderful regional delicacies. I had planned to walk the 20 kilometers back to the train station in Moulins, but Michelle insisted that I allow her to drive me. She wanted to nourish and protect me the way they protect their Black Madonna.

The town of Bresnay was so concerned about preserving their Black Madonna, and safeguarding her from the elements and potential theft, that they created an actual decoy. As if that wasn't enough, they then protected their Black Madonna so well that many of the townspeople didn't even know where she was kept.

Imagine if we cherished and protected all Black women like the town of Bresnay cherishes and protects their Black Madonna.

Imagine a world in which Black women are well fed and well rested.

Imagine a world in which Black women's bodies are seen as vulnerable, human, and worthy of protection.

Imagine a world in which the community anticipates the threats that may harm Black women and then strategically and structurally protects Black women from those potential threats.

Imagine a world in which the community actually cares about the threats that Black women face.

Imagine a world in which the community actually believes Black women when we tell them of the threats we face.

Imagine a world in which Black women are constantly affirmed and told "You're too sacred for this."

Imagine a world in which Black women's illnesses and disabilities are attributed to systemic oppression rather than individual moral failings.

Imagine a world in which white women exert effort and perform labor in support of Black women's rest and well-being instead of the other way around.

Imagine a world in which Black women are not required to be available to meet the needs of everyone around them.

Imagine a world in which everyone doesn't have access to Black women.

Imagine a world in which Black women's skin is never ashy and always moisturized because we actually have ample time for self-care.

Imagine a world in which Black women, especially Black trans women, are truly sacred.

Black Madonna, the ancient Sacred Black Feminine who birthed reality, anoints us to join her in co-birthing this world.

I'm all in. Are you?

ROOTING IN OUR LADY OF DEEP SOIL

Mystic-activism is not for the faint of heart.

Many of us long to be mystic-activists—people who are alert to injustice and fervently devoted to co-creating a world of love, all while embodying infectious hope, affirming the holiness of our enemies, and releasing the outcome of our efforts to Black Madonna. Whew! If you're anything like me, you know that becoming a mystic-activist is a process of daily surrender and reconditioning.

That's why I'm grateful for a contemporary Black Madonna called Our Lady of Deep Soil by artist Victoria Haf, a particularly fecund Black Madonna who is constantly reviving, nourishing, and breathing life. Our Lady of Deep Soil's image invites us on a mystical journey—traversing the infinite Blackness from which she comes; pondering her vulva-like shape and imagining the life that endlessly springs forth from it; spelunking her deep soil like an earthworm and encountering the nutrients, water, oxygen, and minerals that enrich our lives; welcoming the endless reproductivity in the lush vegetation at her feet; and digesting the countless metaphors embedded in her dreamy title.

A large image of Our Lady of Deep Soil hangs in my living room, and I find myself spending time with her most days. When I gaze at the green-hued flora that enrobe her, I feel like I'm lounging in a warm bath dosed with soothing aloe vera as she calms my nerve-racked body. Perhaps her soothing green glow signals a special love for and embrace of the justice advocates, the anxious ones who are alert to the many ways in which this world is broken and whose hearts break too. When we are most connected to our heartbreak, it's difficult to receive Black Madonna's abundance, difficult to remember that she is holding it all so we don't have to.

While we are deep in our heartbreak, Our Lady of Deep Soil invites us into a different reality—one that is abundant, regenerative, creative, and constantly bringing forth life. Even the mushrooms surrounding Our Lady of Deep Soil speak of her ability to turn death and decay into life. When we commune with her, we are ushered into a sacred space that can handle the "death and decay" of the world's most persistent injustices.

I'm slowly learning to embody mystic-activism by regularly rooting in Our Lady of Deep Soil. When I am connected to the abundance, nourishment, and wisdom that she offers, I find myself stepping off my high horse, relinquishing my ego-grip on self-righteous indignation, opening to her universe-bending hope, trusting her with the outcome of my efforts, and feeling even more energized to participate in her restorative plan on her terms, not mine.

This rooting practice involves:

1. Resting

The times are urgent, let us slow down.
— AFRICAN PROVERB

So often, when we are acutely aware of injustice, we try to numb the pain and anxiety by quickly and imprudently reacting to injustice or by rushing on to the next activity. But slowing down just long enough to be present to our experience helps open us to her abundant soil. Even something as simple and expeditious as a one-minute, five-senses practice—in which you simply identify five things you see, four things you feel, three things you hear, two things you smell, and one thing you taste—can help us slow down enough to connect with ourselves and with Our Lady of Deep Soil. Slowing down enables us to be present enough to realize how much we long to be invited into her world of abundance, generativity, and hospitality.

2. Remembering

זָכַר *(zāḵar in Hebrew) means "to remember,*
recall, or call to mind."

In Judaism there's a long tradition of remembering. The sacred texts are full of examples of Jewish people creating monuments in remembrance of what the Divine had done in their lives. As we explored in this chapter, there's a similar tradition in the lineage of Black Madonna. The stories of her miracles are turned into songs and sung from generation to generation, and the titles given to Black Madonnas specifically relate to the ways she has historically participated in the life of the community. So as we root, we engage in the practice of remembering by asking, "What do I *know* is true?" Then we take a moment to reflect on the ways in which Our Lady of Deep Soil has nourished, supported, and empowered us and others in the past.

3. Reassurance

Never underestimate the body's need for reassurance.
— CYNTHIA WINTON-HENRY

It's helpful to be reminded that it's okay to feel anxious and depressed about injustice and that it's human to need to be reassured that we are divinely accompanied. As an embodied practice of reassurance, you can hug or hold a Black Madonna statue—but trees, beloved animals or humans, and pillows are all great candidates for this practice. While you're hugging/holding, it may be helpful to ask yourself:

- What does Black Madonna want to assure me of right now?

- How does this assurance feel in my body? Where do I feel it?

- How does this assurance empower me to follow her arc of the universe?

This rooting practice of resting, remembering, and reassurance takes just a few minutes and is designed to be incorporated into our everyday lives—while drinking our morning coffee, at a long stoplight, while taking public transportation, while washing the dishes. We can return to it as often as we need to as we nurture our practice of mystic-activism.

ENDNOTES

Chapter 1: She Sparks Our Liberation

1. Kelsey Blackwell, *Decolonizing the Body* (Oakland, CA: New Harbinger Publications, 2023), introduction, Kindle.

2. Peter H. Wood, "Stono Rebellion" in *Encyclopedia of African-American Culture and History: The Black Experience in the Americas,* ed. Colin A. Palmer (Macmillan Reference USA, 2006), 2148.

3. Mark M. Smith, *Stono: Documenting and Interpreting a Southern Slave Revolt* (Columbia, SC: University of South Carolina Press, 2005).

4. David Daniels, "African Christianity and Partnership with North American Churches: An Historical Glimpse" in *Anthology of African Christianity*, ed. Isabel Apawo Phiri, Dietrich Werner, Chammah Kaunda, and Kennedy Owino (Oxford, UK: Regnum Books International, 2016), 898–905.

5. William Hart McNichols and Mirabai Starr, *Mother of God Similar to Fire* (Maryknoll, NY: Orbis Books, 2010), introduction, Kindle.

6. Smith, *Stono,* 112.

7. Smith, *Stono,* 113.

8. Clarissa Pinkola Estés, *Untie the Strong Woman: Blessed Mother's Immaculate Love for the Wild Soul* (Louisville, CO: Sounds True, 2017), 150—51.

9. bell hooks and Amalia Mesa-Bains, *Homegrown: Engaged Cultural Criticism* (Oxfordshire, UK: Routledge, 2017), Chapter 2, Kindle.

10. Nadra Nittle, *bell hooks' Spiritual Vision: Buddhist, Christian, and Feminist* (Minneapolis, MN: Fortress Press, 2023), 15.

11. Justin Randolph Thompson, "Nigra Sum" in *Black Madonna—Mark Steven Greenfield*, exh. cat. (Santa Monica, CA: William Turner Gallery, 2020), https://www.williamturnergallery.com/black-madonna.

12. Chanequa Walker-Barnes, *Too Heavy a Yoke: Black Women and the Burden of Strength* (Eugene, OR: Cascade Books, 2014), 142.

13. Mark Steven Greenfield, "The Black Madonna Series" in *Black Madonna—Mark Steven Greenfield*, exh. cat. (Santa Monica, CA: William Turner Gallery 2020), https://www.williamturnergallery.com/black-madonna.

14. Cynthia Dewi Oka, "A Conversation with My Six-Year-Old about Revolution" in *Revolutionary Mothering: Love on the Front Lines*, ed. Alexis Pauline Gumbs, China Martens, and Mai'a Williams (Oakland, CA: PM Press, 2016), 43.

15. Estés, *Untie the Strong Woman,* 197.

Chapter 2: She Has Loved Us Since the Beginning of Time

1. Bayo Akomolafe, "For Those Spirited Away: Making Sanctuary as a Vocation of Exile in Restless Times," virtual lecture, October 9, 2024, posted October 15, 2024, by Institute for Global Citizenship, YouTube, 1:14:46, https://www.youtube.com/watch?v=gEnPt2MKGE8.

2. Ean Begg, *The Cult of the Black Virgin* (London: Penguin Books, 2006), 61.

3. Clarissa Pinkola Estés, *Untie the Strong Woman: Blessed Mother's Immaculate Love for the Wild Soul* (Louisville, CO: Sounds True, 2017), 73.

4. Sheri Parks, *Fierce Angels: Living with a Legacy from the Sacred Dark Feminine to the Strong Black Woman* (Chicago: Lawrence Hill Books, 2013), 13.

5. Parks, *Fierce Angels*, 14.

6. Parks, *Fierce Angels*, 14.

7. Parks, *Fierce Angels*, 17–18.

8. Merlin Stone, *When God Was a Woman* (New York: Harvest, 1976), 22.

9. Stone, *When God Was a Woman*, 13.

10. Parks, *Fierce Angels*, 16.

11. Lucia Chiavola Birnbaum, *Dark Mother: African Origins and Godmothers* (Bloomington, IN: iUniverse, 2002).

12. M. Kate Allen, *Thean Psalter* (Tempe, AZ: Thea Press, 2018), Kindle, Psalm 42.

13. Parks, *Fierce Angels*, 13.

Chapter 3: She Crosses Oceans for Us

1. Nayyiraeh Waheed, "African American II" in *Salt* (self-pub, CreateSpace, 2013), 114.

2. Ócha'ni Lele, *Sacrificial Ceremonies of Santería: A Complete Guide to the Rituals and Practices* (Rochester, VT: Destiny Books, 2012), 94.

3. Lele, *Sacrificial Ceremonies of Santería*, 95.

4. María Elena Díaz, *The Virgin, the King, and the Royal Slaves of El Cobre: Negotiating Freedom in Colonial Cuba, 1670–1780* (Redwood City, CA: Stanford University Press, 2000), 23.

5. Díaz, *The Virgin, the King, and the Royal Slaves of El Cobre*, 113, 99.

6. Díaz, *The Virgin, the King, and the Royal Slaves of El Cobre*, 99.

7. Jadele McPherson, "Eusebia Cosme and El Cobre: Performing Sacred Histories," *ReVista: The Harvard Review of Latin America* 20, no. 2 (2021), accessed October 22, 2025, https://revista.drclas.harvard.edu/eusebia-cosme-and-el-cobre -performing-sacred-histories/.

8. Díaz, *The Virgin, the King, and the Royal Slaves of El Cobre*, 100.

9. Díaz, *The Virgin, the King, and the Royal Slaves of El Cobre*, 107.

10. Díaz, *The Virgin, the King, and the Royal Slaves of El Cobre*, 108.

11. Patricia Monaghan, *Encyclopedia of Goddesses and Heroines* (Novato, CA: New World Library, 2014),15; Monica A. Coleman, "African American Religion and Gender" in *African American Religious Cultures*, ed. Anthony B. Pinn, (New York: Bloomsbury, 2006), 501; Nathaniel Samuel Murrell, *Afro-Caribbean Religions: An Introduction to Their Historical, Cultural, and Sacred Traditions* (Philadelphia, PA: Temple University Press, 2009).

Chapter 4: She Mothers Us into Abundance

1. jessica Care moore, *We Want Our Bodies Back: Poems* (New York: Amistad, 2020), 21.

2. Andre M. Perry, Hannah Stephens, and Manann Donoghoe, "Black Wealth Is Increasing, But So Is the Racial Wealth Gap," Brookings Institute, January 9, 2024, https://www.brookings.edu/articles/black-wealth-is-increasing-but-so -is-the-racial-wealth-gap/.

3. Donna Kate Rushin, "The Bridge Poem," in *This Bridge Called My Back: Writings by Radical Women of Color*, ed. Cherríe Moraga and Gloria Anzaldúa, 4th edition (Albany, NY: SUNY Press, 2015), xxxiii.

4. Sophie Cassagnes-Brouquet, *Vierges Noires* (Arles, France: Éditions du Rouergue, 2000), 130.

5. Renée Merlet, "La Cathédrale de Chartres et ses Origines: à propos de la découverte du puits des Saints-Forts," *Revue archéologique, 41 (*1902): 232–41.

6. Annine van der Meer, *The Black Madonna: From Primal Times to Final Times*, trans. Catriona O'Daly (Pan Sophia Press, 2015), 330.

7. Ean Begg, *The Cult of the Black Virgin* (London: Penguin Books, 2006), 43.

8. Friends of the Labyrinth, "Chartres Labyrinth & Symbolism," accessed October 23, 2025, https://www.labyrinth.org.nz/what-is-a-labyrinth/chartres-labyrinth -and-symbolism/.

9. Regina Renee Nyégbeh, personal communication, May 2, 2025.

10. Nyégbeh, personal communication.

11. M. Kate Allen, *Thean Psalter* (Tempe, AZ: Thea Press, 2018), Kindle, Psalm 18.

12. Begg, *The Cult of the Black Virgin*, 134.

13. Begg, *The Cult of the Black Virgin*, 145.

14. Marcus Bull, *The Miracles of Our Lady of Rocamadour: Analysis and Translation* (Martlesham, Suffolk, UK: Boydell & Brewer Press, 1999), 164–65.

15. Begg, *The Cult of the Black Virgin*, 144.

16. angel Kyodo williams, *Being Black: Zen and the Art of Living with Fearlessness and Grace* (New York: Penguin Compass, 2000), 13–26.

17. Robert Bly and Marion Woodman, *The Maiden King: The Reunion of Masculine and Feminine* (New York: Henry Holt and Company, 1998), 145–46.

18. Begg, *The Cult of the Black Virgin*, 144.

19. "The Labyrinth Locator," accessed October 28, 2025, https://labyrinthlocator.org/.

20. Friends of the Labyrinth, "Chartres Labyrinth & Symbolism."

Chapter 5: She Fiercely Defends Us

1.   Elise Herron, "One of Late Writer Toni Morrison's Most Famous Quotes About Racism Came from a Talk at Portland State University. Listen to It Here," *Willamette Week*, August 7, 2019, https://www.wweek.com/news/2019/08/07/one-of-late-writer-toni-morrisons-most-famous-quotes-about-racism-came-from-a-talk-at-portland-state-university-listen-to-it-here/.

2.   Cecilia M. Dorger, "Studies in the Image of the Madonna Lactans in Late Medieval and Renaissance Italy," Electronic Theses and Dissertations, Paper 367 (2012), accessed October 28, 2025, https://doi.org/10.18297/etd/367.

3.   Michele Chabin, "The Milk Grotto Church Heals Infertile Couples," *National Catholic Register*, September 13, 2003, https://www.ncregister.com/news/the-milk-grotto-church-heals-infertile-couples.

4.   Chabin, "The Milk Grotto Church Heals Infertile Couples."

5.   Dorger, "Studies in the Image of the Madonna Lactans in Late Medieval and Renaissance Italy."

6.   Ella Rozett, Interfaith Mary, accessed September 18, 2025, https://www.interfaithmary.net/black-madonna-index/chatillon-sur-seine.

7.   Pavel Štěpánek, "Tasting the Milk of Celestial Knowledge. Note about the rhetoric of the portrayal of the sacred in Alonso Cano's painting *The Lactation of St. Bernard* (1653–1657) from the National Gallery in Prague" in *The Figurativeness of the Language of Mystical Experience. Particularities and Interpretations*, ed. Antonio Barnés Vázquez and Magda Kučerková (Brno, Czech Republic: Masaryk University Press, 2021), 220–40.

8.   David Gibson, "Jesus was not a bottle baby. What happened to Maria Lactans?," *Commonweal Magazine*, December 11, 2012, https://www.commonwealmagazine.org/jesus-was-not-bottle-baby-what-happened-maria-lactans.

9.   Alfonso X, *Alfonso X, the Learned, 'Cantigas de Santa Maria': An Anthology*, trans. Stephen Parkinson (Cambridge, UK: Modern Humanities Research Association, 2015).

Chapter 6: She Soothes Our Deepest Wounds

1.   Fred Gustafson, *The Black Madonna of Einsiedeln: An Ancient Image for Our Present Time* (Einsiedeln, Switzerland: Daimon Verlag, 2008), 23.

2.   Gustafson, *The Black Madonna of Einsiedeln*, 32.

3.   Clarissa Pinkola Estés, *Untie the Strong Woman: Blessed Mother's Immaculate Love for the Wild Soul* (Louisville, CO: Sounds True, 2017), 150–52.

4.   Marion Woodman and Jill Mellick, *Coming Home to Myself: Reflections for Nurturing a Woman's Body and Soul* (San Francisco: Red Wheel/Weiser, 1998).

5.   Kristen L. Harper, *The Darkness Divine: A Loving Challenge to My Faith* (Boston: Skinner House Books, 2021), Kindle, 16.

6.   Gustafson, *The Black Madonna of Einsiedeln*, 28.

7. Emmanuel Katongole, "Emmanuel Katongole: Lament and Hope in Africa," *Faith & Leadership*, July 25, 2017, https://faithandleadership.com/emmanuel -katongole-lament-and-hope-africa.

8. Gustafson, *The Black Madonna of Einsiedeln*, 55.

9. Gustafson, *The Black Madonna of Einsiedeln*, 57–58.

10. Harper, *The Darkness Divine*.

11. Bayo Akomolafe, "For Those Spirited Away: Making Sanctuary as a Vocation of Exile in Restless Times," virtual lecture, October 9, 2024, posted October 15, 2024, by Institute for Global Citizenship, YouTube, 1:14:46, https://www .youtube.com/watch?v=gEnPt2MKGE8.

12. Ursula K. Le Guin, "A Left-Handed Commencement Address," delivered at Mills College, Oakland, CA, May 22, 1983, https://www.ursulakleguin.com /lefthand-mills-college.

13. Harper, *The Darkness Divine*, 21.

14. Michael Murphy, "The Troubling Past of Forced Sterilization of Black Women and Girls in Mississippi and the South," *Mississippi Free Press*, June 4, 2021, https://www.mississippifreepress.org/the-troubling-past-of-forced-sterilization -of-black-women-and-girls-in-mississippi-and-the-south/.

15. Carla Laroche, "The New Jim and Jane Crow Intersect: Challenges to Defending the Parental Rights of Mothers During Incarceration," *Columbia Journal of Race and Law* 12, no. 1 (2022).

16. Grace Panetta and Barbara Rodriguez, "Case of a Brain-Dead Pregnant Woman Kept on Life Support Is 'Gut-Wrenching,' Advocates Say," *Louisiana Illuminator*, May 18, 2025, https://lailluminator.com/2025/05/18/pregnant-life-support/; Jennifer Bellamy, "Infant of Georgia Woman Who Carried Baby while Brain Dead Still Fighting for His Life," *11 Alive*, August 26, 2025.

17. Donna L. Hoyert, "Health E-Stat 100: Maternal Mortality Rates in the United States, 2023," CDC National Center for Health Statistics, https://www.cdc.gov /nchs/data/hestat/maternal-mortality/2023/maternal-mortality-rates-2023.htm.

18. Gustafson, *The Black Madonna of Einsiedeln*, 144.

19. Chanequa Walker-Barnes, *Too Heavy a Yoke: Black Women and the Burden of Strength* (Eugene, OR: Cascade Books, 2014).

20. Upile Chisala, *A Fire Like You* (Kansas City, MO: Andrews McMeel Publishing, 2020).

21. Harper, *The Darkness Divine*, 23.

22. Harper, *The Darkness Divine*, 44.

Chapter 7: She Fortifies Our Hope

1. Alexis Pauline Gumbs, "Prophecy in the Present Tense: Harriet Tubman, the Combahee Pilgrimage, and Dreams Coming True," *Meridians* 12, no. 2 (2014), 142–52.

2. The Memorare," *Vatican News*, accessed September 26, 2026, https://www .vaticannews.va/en/prayers/the-memorare.html.

3.   Taylor Tripodi, "Why Adoration Is Essential for the Soul and Body," *Ascension Press*, January 4, 2019, https://media.ascensionpress.com /2019/01/04/why-adoration-is-essential-for-soul-and-body/.

4.   Eileen G'Sell, "An Afro-Surrealist Project Deifies God-Like Bodies of Color," *Hyperallergic*, July 12, 2018, https://hyperallergic.com/450970/damon-davis -darker-gods-in-the-garden-of-the-low-hanging-heavens-luminary-arts/.

5.   "Balata Camp," United Nations Relief and Works Agency accessed September 26, 2025, https://www.unrwa.org/where-we-work/west-bank/balata-camp.

6.   C. Daryl Cameron and B. Keith Paine, "Escaping Affect: How Motivated Emotion Regulation Creates Insensitivity to Mass Suffering" *Journal of Personality and Social Psychology, 100*, no. 1 (2011), 1–15.

7.   Jeremiah Wright, "The Audacity to Hope," *Preaching Today*, 1990, accessed October 28, 2025, https://www.preachingtoday.com/sermons/sermons/2010 /july/audacityofhope.html.

8.   Howard Thurman, *Deep River and The Negro Spiritual Speaks of Life and Death* (Richmond, IN: Friends United Press, 1975).

9.   Andrew Harvey, *The Return of the Mother* (Berkeley,CA: Frog Books, 1995), 170.

10.   Justin Randolph Thompson, "Nigra Sum" in *Black Madonna—Mark Steven Greenfield*, exh. cat. (Santa Monica, CA: William Turner Gallery, 2020).

11.   Thompson, "Nigra Sum."

Chapter 8: She Anoints Us to Embody Her in the World

1.   "Ethnicity in the Philippines (2020 Census of Population and Housing)," Philippine Statistics Authority, updated July 4, 2023, https://psa.gov.ph/content /ethnicity-philippines-2020-census-population-and-housing.

2.   Mary Mijares, "Indigenous Women in the Philippines Fight for Their Rights," *The Organization for World Peace*, August 25, 2021, https://theowp.org /indigenous-women-in-the-philippines-fight-for-their-rights.

3.   Oliver Baccay, "Itawes: The People Across the Cagayan River," Philippine Information Agency, April 30, 2024, https://mirror.pia.gov.ph/features /2024/04/30/itawes-the-people-across-the-cagayan-river.

4.   "Top 10 Countries with Large Catholic Population," Catholic World Mission, https://www.catholicworldmission.org/post/top-10-countries -with-large-catholic-population.

5.   Aaron Veloso, "Our Lady of Piat: Yena Tam Ngamin, Mother of Us All," *Dominus Est*, updated June 28, 2023, https://www.dominusest.ph/post /our-lady-of-piat-yena-tam-ngamin-mother-of-us-all.

6.   Veloso, "Our Lady of Piat.

7.   Immaculee Ilibagiza, *Our Lady of Kibeho: Mary Speaks to the World from the Heart of Africa* (Carlsbad, CA: Hay House, 2010), Introduction, Kindle.

8.   Michelle Wolff, "Madonna and Child of Soweto: Black Life Beyond Apartheid and Democracy," *Political Theology* 19, no. 7 (2018), 576.

9. Alessandra Belloni, *Healing Journeys with the Black Madonna: Chants, Music, and Sacred Practices of the Great Goddess* (Rochester, VT: Bear & Company, 2019), Chapter 4, Kindle.

10. Emma Cieslik, "The Madonna di Montevergine, mother of LGBTQ Catholics," *U.S. Catholic*, November 9, 2023, "https://uscatholic.org/articles/202311/the-madonna-di-montevergine-mother-of-lgbtq-catholics/.

11. Terry Rey, *Our Lady of Class Struggle: The Cult of the Virgin Mary in Haiti* (Trenton, NJ: Africa World Press, 1998).

12. Alfonso X, *Alfonso X, the Learned, 'Cantigas de Santa Maria': An Anthology*, trans. Stephen Parkinson (Cambridge, UK: Modern Humanities Research Association, 2015), 65.

13. Alfonso X, *Alfonxo X*, 64.

14. Alfonso X, *Alfonxo X*, 65.

15. Arundhati Roy, *War Talk* (Boston: South End Press, 2003).

16. Curtiss DeYoung, *Living Faith: How Faith Inspires Social Justice* (Minneapolis, MN: Fortress Press, 2007).

17. Marcia Bjornerud, *Timefulness: How Thinking Like a Geologist Can Help Save the World* (Princeton, NJ: Princeton University Press, 2018).

ACKNOWLEDGMENTS

This book is a cosmic collaboration with my ancestors, whose voices, gifts, and stories keep my soul's blood pumping.

I honor my paternal great-grandfather, Bishop E.E. Cleveland, whose 1960s Berkeley church hosted the Black Panther Party's community programs. I carry his legacy of spiritual activism within me.

I honor my paternal great-aunt, Bishop Ernestine Cleveland Reems, who refused to allow patriarchy to silence her prophetic voice and stifle her blazing spiritual leadership. I carry her holy audacity and oratorical flair within me.

I honor my paternal grandfather, Dr. John Cleveland, a trailblazing founder of multiple Afrocentric educational institutions. I carry his intellectual and visionary gifts within me.

I honor my maternal grandfather, Bishop William H. Allen, whose gentle demeanor and easy smile showed me that meekness can be mighty too. I carry his pastoral heart within me.

I honor my middle namesake and maternal great-aunt, Sara Jordan Powell, a legendary gospel singer who fervently championed my initiation into Black Madonna. I carry her creative and radically inclusive spirituality within me.

So many wonderful people poured their passion and skills into this book. Thank you to my agent, Chris Park, whose wisdom and pluck always lift me and my work. Thank you to the Hay House editorial team and collaborators: Anna Cooperberg and Patty Gift for believing in and nurturing my vision, Nicolette Salamanca Young for generously and artfully guiding this book into life, Adaobi Obi Tulton for being the sister-editor of my dreams, and Sheridan McCarthy for pouring love into the details.

I am also immensely grateful to the robust community of beloveds who collectively mother me: Pixie, Adriana, Jacyntha, Mirabai, Matthew, Andrew, Andrea, Nadya, Tiffany, Marlena, Charlotte, Debra, Goddexx, Uncle Greg, Lisa, Renee, SK, Mardi, Barbara, Rachel, Curtiss, Caille, Kim, Dee, Becca, Marque, Stacy, Cristin, John, Des, and Nate. I experience Black Madonna's wisdom and love in each of you. Deep, deep bow.

Enfin Notre Dame—La Noire: Je vous fais confiance.

ABOUT THE COVER ILLUSTRATION AND ARTIST

Black artists are my most treasured teachers. As I wrote in *God Is a Black Woman*, "Imagination is theology; we can only believe what we can imagine." Black art floods me with holy audacity and sends my spiritual imagination soaring beyond the limits that society has tried to instill.

Years ago, as I journeyed toward Black Madonna and began to experience the spirituality that I present in this book, I longed for more contemporary images of her. Although I love the ancient statues and icons, I knew that present-day representations of Black Madonna would nourish my spiritual imagination as I explored how she accompanies and empowers us today.

I commissioned Afro-Filipina artist Laylie Frazier to reimagine 11 medieval Black Madonna statues as 21st-century icons with a variety of skin tones, gender expressions, age, and body types. One of Frazier's Black Madonnas is on the cover of this book. I see her as a queen, liberator, superhero, mother, and community activist. She is vigorously present, and her gaze is unswerving. She is the icon of resistance and nourisher of souls who dwells among us. Always.

I am immensely grateful to Laylie for illuminating my spiritual imagination and generously sharing her creative gifts.

⋆ ⋆ ⋆

Laylie Frazier is a Black and Filipina artist from Houston, Texas. She loves using a mix of warm colors and textures to create powerfully emotive portraits. Laylie is currently illustrating middle grade and young adult covers for publishing as well as working in advertising. The first picture book she illustrated, *I See Color*, written by Valerie Bolling and Kailei Pew, was released by HarperCollins in 2024.

Website: **ukelaylie.myportfolio.com**

ABOUT THE AUTHOR

Christena Cleveland, PhD, is a social psychologist, public theologian, mystic-activist, and author of several books, including *God Is a Black Woman*. She is the founder of the Black Madonna Freedom School, which nurtures courageous and compassionate people who are uprooting white patriarchal religious conditioning in themselves and their communities, while skillfully planting intersectional divine feminine wisdom.

A weaver of Black liberation and the divine feminine, Christena is a sought-after speaker and facilitator who integrates psychology, theology, storytelling, and somatics as she guides people of all races and genders into freedom, wholeness, and embodied justice. She holds a PhD in social psychology from the University of California, Santa Barbara, a BA from Dartmouth College, where she double majored in sociology and psychological and brain sciences. An award-winning scholar, her work has been featured in a number of major media outlets, including the History Channel, PBS, *Essence* magazine, *The Washington Post*, NPR, and BBC Radio.

A bona fide tea snob, lover of Black art, and Ólafur Arnalds superfan, Christena makes her home in Minneapolis, Minnesota.

Websites: **christenacleveland.com**
and **blackmadonnaschool.com**

Hay House Titles of Related Interest

YOU CAN HEAL YOUR LIFE, the movie,
starring Louise Hay & Friends
(available as an online streaming video)
www.hayhouse.com/louise-movie

THE SHIFT, the movie,
starring Dr. Wayne W. Dyer
(available as an online streaming video)
www.hayhouse.com/the-shift-movie

*AFRICAN GODDESS INITIATION: Sacred Rituals for
Self-Love, Prosperity, and Joy* by Abiola Abrams

BLACK GODDESS WITHIN ORACLE: A 44-Card Deck and Guidebook
by Giavanni Washington, PhD, and Marla Warner

*BLACK MOON LILITH RISING: How to Unlock the Power of
the Dark Divine Feminine Through Astrology* by Adama Sesay

*THE SPIRIT OF HARRIET TUBMAN:
Awakening from the Underground* by Spring Washam

All of the above are available at your local bookstore,
or may be ordered by contacting Hay House (see next page).

We hope you enjoyed this Hay House book. If you'd like to receive our online catalog featuring additional information on Hay House books and products, or if you'd like to find out more about the Hay Foundation, please contact:

Hay House LLC, P.O. Box 5100, Carlsbad, CA 92018-5100
(760) 431-7695 or (800) 654-5126
www.hayhouse.com® • www.hayfoundation.org

———

Published in Australia by:
Hay House Australia Publishing Pty Ltd
18/36 Ralph St., Alexandria NSW 2015
Phone: +61 (02) 9669 4299
www.hayhouse.com.au

Published in the United Kingdom by:
Hay House UK Ltd
1st Floor, Crawford Corner,
91–93 Baker Street, London W1U 6QQ
Phone: +44 (0)20 3927 7290
www.hayhouse.co.uk

Published in India by:
Hay House Publishers (India) Pvt Ltd
Muskaan Complex, Plot No. 3,
B-2, Vasant Kunj, New Delhi 110 070
Phone: +91 11 41761620
www.hayhouse.co.in

———

Let Your Soul Grow

Experience life-changing transformation—one video at a time—with guidance from the world's leading experts.

www.healyourlifeplus.com

TRANSFORM YOUR DAY— ANYTIME, ANYWHERE

With the **Empower You** Unlimited Audio *App*

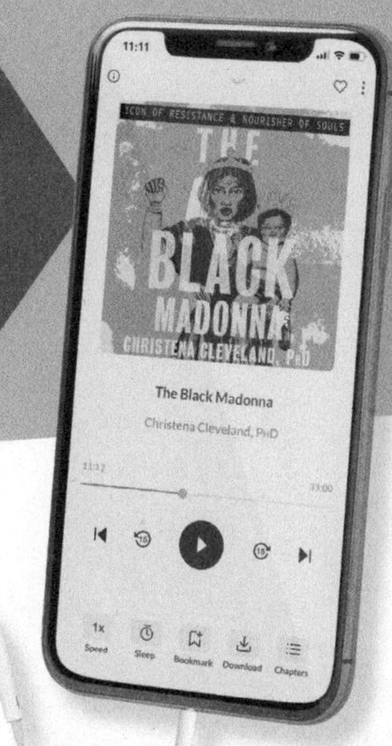

> **★★★★★ Life changing.**
> My fav app on my entire phone, hands down! – Gigi

Unlimited access to the entire Hay House audio library!

You'll get:

- 600+ soul-stirring **audiobooks** to expand your mind
- 1,000+ **meditations** for restful sleep, morning focus, and gentle healing
- Bite-sized audios **under 20 minutes**—perfect for busy days
- **Exclusive talks** you won't find anywhere else
- **Daily affirmations**
- Fresh content added **every week** to fuel your journey

> Driving, yard work, and housework have been **transformed!** – Ruffles27

Scan the QR code to start listening or visit **hayhouse.com/unlimited**